Irène Joliot-Curie (1897-1956)

An Hachette UK Company
www.hachette.co.uk

First published in Great Britain in 2018 by
Cassell Illustrated, a division of
Octopus Publishing Group Ltd
Carmelite House
50 Victoria Embankment
London EC4Y 0DZ
www.octopusbooks.co.uk

Distributed in the US by Hachette Book Group
1290 Avenue of the Americas
4th and 5th Floors, New York, NY 10104

Distributed in Canada by Canadian Manda Group
664 Annette St.
Toronto, Ontario, Canada M6S 2C8

ISBN 978 1 78840 042 8

Printed and bound in China
10 9 8 7 6 5 4 3 2 1

Commissioning Editor: Romilly Morgan
Managing Editor: Sybella Stephens
Copy Editor: Linda Schofield
Assistant Editor: Ellie Corbett
Art Director and Designer: Yasia Williams-Leedham
Illustrators: Allegra Lockstadt, Sara Netherway,
    Lauren Simkin Berke, Hannah Berman,
    María Hergueta, Miriam Castillo, Marcela Quiroz,
    Shreyas Krishnan, Laura Inksetter, Tanya Heidrich,
    Winnie T Frick, Hélène Baum, Bodil Jane
Production Controller: Meskerem Berhane

FORGOTTEN WOMEN
The Scientists

ZING TSJENG

CASSELL
ILLUSTRATED

INTRODUCTION 6

n 1983 a researcher named David Wade Chambers developed the Draw-a-Scientist Test. It was a simple way to work out when children began developing an image of the typical scientist in their heads. Did they see them as bespectacled geniuses in lab coats? Wild-eyed sorcerers with frizzy hair and potions? Or shy bookworms with their nose buried in a pile of academic papers?

Over the next 11 years, Chambers administered tests to more than 4,000 children between the ages of 5 and 11. The results were singularly depressing: of the thousands of drawings produced, only 28 featured female scientists. These were all drawn by girls, who made up 49 per cent of the study; there wasn't a single picture of a woman drawn by a boy. In other words, in the eyes of an average child, a scientist was far likelier to be a bearded figure shouting something like "Eureka!" and "I've got it!" than – a female.[1]

This isn't a slight on the schoolchildren of Montreal, Quebec, where the majority of the study's subjects came from. But if children are supposed to be our future, then the future – at least when it comes to science – is looking very male indeed.

According to the Women in Science and Engineering (WISE) campaign, women currently occupy just 21.1 per cent of the total STEM (science, technology, engineering and mathematics) jobs in the UK.[2] Things are only fractionally better in the US: although women make up about 50 per cent of the workforce,

statistics for 2011 from the United States Department of Commerce show that they take up less than 25 per cent of STEM positions.[3]

To be fair, women have been shut out of typical routes to scientific careers for a very long time. Most institutions of higher education did not begin to accept women until the 20th century. Magdalene College at the University of Cambridge – which counts a Nobel-winning physicist among its alumni – waited until 1986 to admit female students, reportedly prompting its men to hold a funeral procession, complete with coffin, to mourn the death of the college.[4]

These elite schools and academies were – and still are – seen as the gatekeepers of scientific accomplishment: training ground, career-making research centre and intellectual hothouse all in one. And in the past they were about as open-minded as an 11-year-old Montreal schoolchild when it came to who could pass through their doors.

So does this mean that the history books are totally empty of women making earth-shattering discoveries, teasing out scientific truths or publishing bombshell revelations about the inner workings of the universe? Of course not.

Can't get into university? No problem. In the 18th century, French mathematician Sophie Germain (see page 172) adopted a male *nom de plume* – Monsieur Le Blanc – so she could obtain the lecture notes. Can't speak to your academic peers because of their penchant for socializing at all-male clubs? Émilie du Châtelet (see page 156) dressed up in male drag so that she could stroll into Café Gradot to discuss equations.

If you look even further back, you can find women in antiquity and medieval times who were scientific trailblazers in their own right, and whose contributions to their field are still alive and well. Maria the Jewess (also known as Maria the Prophetess, see page 176) was so highly regarded as a chemist and alchemist in the ancient world that she was rumoured to have discovered the Philosopher's Stone itself, but the innovation for which she is best known is the bain-marie, or the double boiler, which is still used in kitchens today.

Even longer ago, Tapputi (see page 140) – the chemist by royal appointment of the ancient Babylonian court – distilled and extracted chemicals for use in perfumes and unguents in Mesopotamia, the cradle of civilization. And four centuries after the birth of Christ, the Greek doctor Aspasia (see page 68) was pioneering gynaecological and surgical techniques that any doctor will find familiar today, including a way to rotate a breech baby for birth.

But if you had asked me to draw a picture of a scientist as a child, I wouldn't have drawn any of these women. In all honesty, I would probably have drawn a picture of a man. You see, even though I had been taught by female science teachers and went to an all-girls' elementary school, I had still absorbed and digested the stereotype of what a scientist *should* look like. By the age of 14, you were most likely to spot me in a chemistry or mathematics class, throwing my hands up in the air and saying, "I just can't do it," and my teachers affirming,

"Well, that is the one thing you definitely got right."

Shamefully, I still carry the remnants of that attitude with me now. If I offer to split a bill at a restaurant, I'm scared that even working it out on my phone, let alone in my head, would show me up as mathematically incapable. Yet every time I've *had* to do it, I've surprised myself with how capable I can be.

I suspect that's true for a lot of girls in science classes. Girls and boys are not born able to wield a Bunsen burner or a calculator with any more or less competence than the other, but adults tend to have lower expectations of the girls' abilities. The girls then internalize these lessons over time, becoming a little less confident and a little less outspoken with every passing comment, until the words come tumbling out of their own mouths: "Don't ask me! I can't do it!"

Forgotten Women: The Scientists has been a way of re-educating myself and to show that there were plenty of women who couldn't just "do" it: they did it exceedingly well, and better than anybody else, often while confronting incredible levels of sexism and at exceedingly high personal cost.

History is full of brilliant women who were forced to accept unpaid jobs as volunteers or assistants just to get their foot in the lab door. Or who were made to resign or step down from their positions after getting married (the logic presumably being that they were better suited to wearing aprons than they were lab coats and goggles).

And when these women made an incredible discovery of their own – the kind that cracks open the field of nuclear fission, for instance – they were often conned out of their rightful acknowledgment. The praise was redirected to male collaborators, research partners and – in more than one case – husbands.

It's little wonder that when British astronomer Cecilia Payne-Gaposchkin looked back on her decades-long career in science, she didn't mince her words: "A **woman knows the frustration of belonging to a minority group. We may not actually be a minority, but we are certainly disadvantaged.**"[5]

Working with The New Historia at the New School, Parsons, we picked 48 women to profile for each book in the *Forgotten Women* series: 48, because that's the total number of women who have won the Nobel Prize between its inception in 1901 and 2017, when its latest batch of winners was announced at the time of writing. That's 48 out of 911 Nobel Laureates in total, going back all the way to the beginning of the 20th century. Some of those women's stories are detailed here. Others, like DNA crystallographer Rosalind Franklin (see page 120) and nuclear physicist Lise Meitner (see page 132), were arguably cheated out of their Nobel.

Trawling through the length and breadth of scientific history to choose the women in *The Scientists* was a daunting – and humbling – task. I have attempted to include a truly diverse and representative mix of scientists from all over the world. However, there's no getting away from the fact that science is just as bad on ethnic diversity as it is on gender equality. Privileged women in the West were often the first to benefit from new scientific opportunities: you just need to look at the West Computers (see page 191) to see an example of where black women were employed at the US space agency only after their white counterparts were admitted. The women who battled the interlocking foes of sexism, racism and class-based prejudice are those I most admire, but every person in *The Scientists* is worthy of praise. Their resistance is illustrated not only by their impressive achievements, but also in the tiny details of their lives, which were the things that brought me the most pleasure to research and write about: radio astronomy trailblazer Ruby Payne-Scott's (see page 33) campaign of stubbornness in wearing shorts to her scandalized office, for instance; or inventor Mary Beatrice Davidson Kenner (see page 180) checking persistently at the US patent office to see if any of her ideas had been patented (she was aged 12); or even Wangari Maathai's (see page 60) brisk assessment of her husband when he requested a divorce: "I should have known that ambition and success were not to be expected in an African woman."

These women live on in their contributions to science, but it's these rich and complex stories of human achievement that have been minimized, sidelined or struck off the page completely. This book is an attempt to wrestle the spotlight back onto these unknown heroes. So the next time a child draws a picture of a scientist, they'll have a little more imagination than just a bearded guy shouting "Gadzooks!"

The earth &
the universe

he era of human computers didn't begin with the West Computers or the Bletchleyettes (see pages 191 and 160). Toward the end of the 19th century, Harvard College Observatory drafted in dozens of women to take on one of the most unique mathematical computing jobs in its 178-year history: to unravel the mysteries of the heavens by calculating the positions of the stars.

The work was less glamorous than it sounded. Thanks to new photographic technology, astronomers were able to capture images of the night sky onto glass plates. The problem, however, was that there was far too much data and too few people to analyse it. Observatory director Edward Charles Pickering (1846–1919) had an unusual solution: he employed a team of women to do it.

At the time, bright and talented graduates were emerging from America's newly founded women's colleges – such as Vassar College in upstate New York – and on the hunt for employment prospects that offered a little more excitement than working as a schoolteacher or running a household. Being a computer was as good as it got, even if they were paid far less than their male colleagues at 25 to 30 cents an hour. But it wasn't just middle-class educated women who were offered a chance at classifying the stars; there were also uneducated women like Williamina Fleming (1857–1911), a Dundee-born single mother and housemaid whose aptitude for computing led Pickering to promote her from cleaning his rooms to computing his plates.

The Harvard Computers (1881–1919) – or, as they more rudely began to be known at the time, Pickering's Harem – worked in the library next to the observatory. The process of measuring the brightness of the stars and their positions in the sky required painstaking attention to detail and utmost concentration. Though the work was considered boring and tedious – hence why women were landed with it –

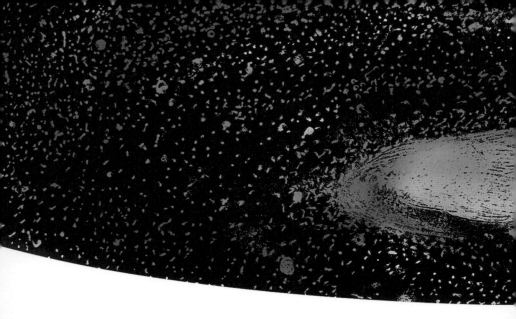

it was also a lot less straightforward than it seemed. Most plates simply revealed dark splodges of dots against the glass. With the careful application of mathematical formulae, the women could work out the coordinates of the stars and their brightness. The northern and southern skies had never been mapped in their entirety before. The Harvard College Observatory, with its immense collection of plates, stood the best chance of doing it, and it couldn't have made any progress without its computers.

Then came another challenge: how should they categorize these celestial bodies? Wellesley College graduate Annie Jump Cannon (1863–1941) created the Harvard Classification Scheme, which sorts the stars based on qualities such as their colour and temperature. As Cannon put it: "It was almost as if the distant stars had really acquired speech, and were able to tell of their constitution and physical condition."[1] Her system is still used by astronomers today. Cannon and another computer, Henrietta Swan Leavitt (1868–1921), were both deaf; in Cannon's case, this proved advantageous when she wanted to concentrate at work, as she would simply remove her hearing aid to block out the noises of the outside world.

Even though none of them – barring Cannon – were ever allowed to use the mighty Harvard telescope known as the Great Refractor, the computers were on the cutting edge of astronomical discovery. Fleming, for instance, catalogued more than 10,000 stars and

was the first to spot the Horsehead Nebula, some 1,500 miles from earth. However, initial publications of the finding missed out her name completely. (Subsequent catalogues, thankfully, rectified the mistake.) In 1899 she became the Curator of astronomical photographs and was one of the few computers to be appointed to a professional position at Harvard. Leavitt, on the other hand, realized that some stars pulsate with consistent brightness, making these so-called Cepheid variables solid benchmarks for calculating distances across space: a method that Edwin Hubble relied on to prove that the universe goes beyond our own paltry galaxy. In this way, the findings made by the Harvard Computers were truly revolutionary.

Harvard continued to use photographic plates until the 1990s, when digital cameras supplanted the old way of doing things. But the 500,000 glass plates that the computers once pored over still reside at the university, along with 118 boxes of notes and logbooks recently unearthed by the curator of the Harvard-Smithsonian Center for Astrophysics. Together, they constitute a perfect record of what the night sky looked like a century ago, and of the women who sat in the small room next to Harvard's telescope, deciphering the secrets of the universe. In 2005 the Center began cleaning and digitizing each glass plate for its archive. At the time of writing, more than 207,000 images have been preserved.

nge Lehmann (1888–1993) experienced her first earthquake in Denmark when she was a teenager. On the Copenhagen street where she was born and raised, a slow but unmistakable rumble under her feet shook the floors of the Lehmann family home, and a lamp hanging from the ceiling began to swing back and forth. "It was very strange," she later recalled. "This was my only experience with an earthquake until I became a seismologist 20 years later."[2]

The epicentre of the quake was never discovered. Denmark is not known for seismic activity due to its distance from any major fault lines; when earthquakes do occur in Europe, they tend to afflict Mediterranean countries such as Italy and Greece. Lehmann was among the many Danes left baffled by the mysterious tremor, but she was probably the only one who went on to become a scientist whose discoveries paved the way to a better understanding of them.

Lehmann was born in 1888 into a highly respected middle-class family of academics, engineers and bankers in Østerbro, the neighbourhood between Copenhagen's three lakes and the sea. Her parents sent her to an especially progressive co-educational school, where, as Lehmann characterized it: "No difference between the intellect of boys and girls was recognized, a fact that brought some disappointments later in life when I had to recognize that this was not the general attitude."[3] Lehmann's route to seismology was circuitous at best; she quit her mathematics degree at the University of Copenhagen due to illness and worked in an actuary's office for some years, before finally graduating in 1920 and getting a job as an assistant to a professor of actuarial science.

Three years into her post, she was hired as an assistant by Niels Erik Nørlund, the director of the Gradmålingen, a scientific institute that was later incorporated into

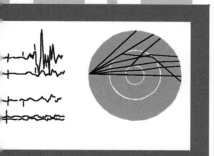

the Royal Danish Geodetic Institute. Nørlund was a mathematician, but he had embarked on an ambitious mission to construct seismological stations in Denmark and Greenland. Along with three young men, Lehmann set to work installing seismographs, despite the fact that she had never seen one before. In fact, Lehmann was pretty much learning as she went along; she tore through seismology books and essentially taught herself everything she needed to know. She wasn't Denmark's only female seismologist; she was its only one, full stop. It is little wonder that the Institute had promoted her to be the head of its seismology department by 1928.

In the early part of the 20th century, geophysicists thought that a molten core lay at the centre of earth, encircled by a solid mantle and then a crust. According to this theory, a certain kind of seismic wave known as P-waves – the kind that a seismograph registers first during an earthquake – would be deflected by the liquid core. But a massive earthquake in New Zealand in 1929 left Lehmann perplexed. A few P-waves had actually been registered at other seismological stations.

As her nephew Niles Groes later remembered, Lehamann left no stone unturned when it came to attacking the mysteries of her field:

"I remember Inge one Sunday in her beloved garden...with a big table filled with cardboard oatmeal boxes. In the boxes were cardboard cards with information on earthquakes... all over the world. This was before computer processing was available, but the system was the same. With her cardboard cards and her oatmeal boxes, Inge registered the velocity of propagation of the earthquakes to all parts of the globe. By means of this information, she deduced new theories of the inner parts of the Earth."[4]

What Lehmann discovered literally turned seismology upside down. According to her calculations, the earth was actually hiding a solid innermost core within its molten centre and this was what the P-waves were bouncing off. "The existence of a small solid core in the innermost part of the earth was seen to result in waves emerging at distances where it had not been possible to predict their presence," she declared.[5] This wasn't the only discovery she made; in 1954 she also noticed that there was a 50-kilometre (31-mile) area buried some 190 kilometres (120 miles) into the earth where seismic waves actually increase in velocity: a mystery known in seismic terms as a discontinuity.

Lehmann remained at the Royal Danish Geodetic Institute for the rest of her life and was still investigating the workings of the earth into her seventies. In 1971 the American Geophysical Union awarded her its highest honour, the William Bowie Medal. When she received the prize, Lehmann was described as "a master of a black art for which no amount of computerization is likely to be a complete substitute."[6] If you needed proof of that, you can just look to the fact that scientists still haven't cracked the Lehmann discontinuity: the seismic quirk that takes its name from the woman who discovered it.

hen children look toward the sky at night and at the stars peeking through the clouds, they may ask questions such as "What are stars?" and "What are they made of?" For the early part of the 20th century, scientists simply didn't know. Many theorized that the stars were made of pretty much the same minerals and elements found in the earth's crust, like silicon and iron. The genius of **Cecilia Payne-Gaposchkin** (1900–1979) was to demonstrate that this was substantively wrong, and in the process she turned the universe upside down.

When Payne-Gaposchkin was five years old, she too looked up at the sky. While on a walk with her mother in Boddington Wood, Buckinghamshire, England, she caught a glimpse of a shooting star. Payne-Gaposchkin's mother taught her a rhyme to remember its name: "As we were walking home that night / We saw a shining meteorite."[7] Payne-Gaposchkin was entranced by the sight of this luminous star appearing to tumble from the heavens.

That night set her on course to become one of the world's pre-eminent astronomers, but when she looked back at her 50-year career, she simply spoke of her unexpected delight at having so dramatically expanded mankind's scientific understanding of space. "I was not consciously aiming at the point I finally reached," she wrote in her autobiography, *The Dyer's Hand*. "I simply went on plodding, rewarded by the beauty of the scenery, towards an unexpected goal."[8]

In her words, Payne-Gaposchkin was "dowdy and studious" as a young woman.[9] She agonized over dances and social events, and was keener on books than boys. ("Fancy!" one of her brother's friends once remarked. "A girl who *reads Plato for pleasure!*"[10]) She was keenly aware that her brother was favoured above the girls in the family, for every effort was made to get him into Oxford. Payne-Gaposchkin, who had her heart set on Cambridge, had to manage it herself by winning a scholarship to Newnham College.

At Cambridge, women were sequestered in separate colleges and segregated from men in lecture theatres. They were even paired off with each other in the lab. But when Payne-Gaposchkin travelled to the Harvard College Observatory for a doctoral degree in astronomy, she

was thrilled that her colleagues there treated her as a fellow scientist; they walked the streets of Cambridge, Massachusetts, and loitered in restaurants arguing passionately about the composition of the universe. "We met as equals; nobody descended to me on account of sex or youth... We were scientists, we were scholars," she said, adding pointedly, "neither of these words has a gender."[11]

Payne-Gaposchkin was one of the few female scholars at the Harvard College Observatory, though she crossed paths with many of the women computers tasked with number-crunching duties there (see page 14). These women had classified hundreds of thousands of stars according to their spectral characteristics, and Payne-Gaposchkin was determined to find out how these related to their actual temperature and composition. "There followed months, almost a year as I remember it, of utter bewilderment," she recalled.[12] But by carefully applying Indian physicist Meghnad Saha's equation of ionization, she was able to link the spectral patterns witnessed by the computers and other astronomers to different temperature ranges. "Two years of estimation, plotting, calculation and the work I had planned was done," she wrote. "I had determined a stellar temperature scale and had measured the astrophysical abundance of the chemical elements."[13]

What she eventually discovered was nothing less than an answer to the burning question: What are the stars made of? She suggested that the stars were overwhelmingly composed of hydrogen and helium in vast quantities: a fact which we now know to be true. But her advisor at the time, American astronomer Henry Norris Russell, believed her results were wildly off and she removed her groundbreaking conclusion on his advice.

Despite this, Payne-Gaposchkin's dissertation, *Stellar Atmospheres*, was praised by Otto Struve and Velta Zebergs, authors of *Astronomy of the 20th Century* (1962), as "the most brilliant PhD thesis ever written in astronomy."[14] All 600 copies of the resulting monograph sold out and she entered J M Cattell's *American Men of Science* as its youngest ever astronomer of note.

But this was 1925 and the path ahead for a female scientist did not run smoothly. Payne-Gaposchkin began teaching at Harvard, but the president of the university said expressly that she would not be appointed to an official post as long as he was still in office. Despite teaching a full course load, she was listed as a "technical assistant" and was underpaid. "I was paid so little that I was ashamed to admit it to my relations in England," she wrote. "They thought I was coining money in a land of millionaires."[15]

Between 1932 and 1933, three of Payne-Gaposchkin's close friends passed away and left her bereft. "I made a silent resolve," she said later. "I would open my heart to the world, I would embrace life and do my part as a human being."[16] She embarked on a grand tour of observatories in Europe as part of her new adventurousness.

Payne-Gaposchkin, who had her head stuck in her books and was oblivious to the mounting tensions in Europe, received a rude shock when she visited the great observatory in Pulkovo, Russia, only to find that the director was forced to steal wood from his neighbour's fences to keep the fire in their office burning. At an astronomy conference in Göttingen, Germany, she received another surprise when a shy Russian astronomer named Sergei Gaposchkin slid a note into her hand. He was exiled from the Soviet Union but was growing increasingly terrified of Nazi persecution in Germany. Would she help him escape to America?

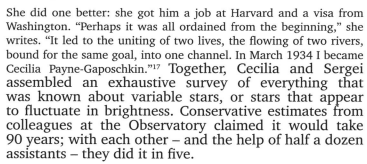

She did one better: she got him a job at Harvard and a visa from Washington. "Perhaps it was all ordained from the beginning," she writes. "It led to the uniting of two lives, the flowing of two rivers, bound for the same goal, into one channel. In March 1934 I became Cecilia Payne-Gaposchkin."[17] Together, Cecilia and Sergei assembled an exhaustive survey of everything that was known about variable stars, or stars that appear to fluctuate in brightness. Conservative estimates from colleagues at the Observatory claimed it would take 90 years; with each other – and the help of half a dozen assistants – they did it in five.

Over the next few decades, they would publish and co-author many papers and books together, and Cecilia was finally given her due when she was appointed chairman of the Department of Astronomy in 1956. Her radical conclusions about the cosmic make-up of the stars was finally proven right: we now know that our galaxy is 74 per cent hydrogen, 24 per cent helium and the remaining 2 per cent other elements.

In her memoirs, Payne-Gaposchkin said that she was often asked by young women for careers advice, which she was happy to give: "Here it is, *valeat quantum*. Do not undertake a scientific career for fame or money...Undertake it only if nothing else will satisfy you; for nothing else is probably what you will receive. Your reward will be the widening of the horizon as you climb. And if you achieve that reward you will ask for no other."[18]

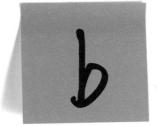

efore she died at the tragically young age of 29, **Wang Zhenyi** (1768–1797) chose poetry to declare: "It's made to believe / Women are the same as Men; / Are you not convinced / Daughters can also be heroic?"[19] It is an apt verse to describe one of the greatest scholars of China's Qing dynasty: a largely self-taught woman who wrote papers on everything from trigonometry to astronomy, as well as poetic verse.

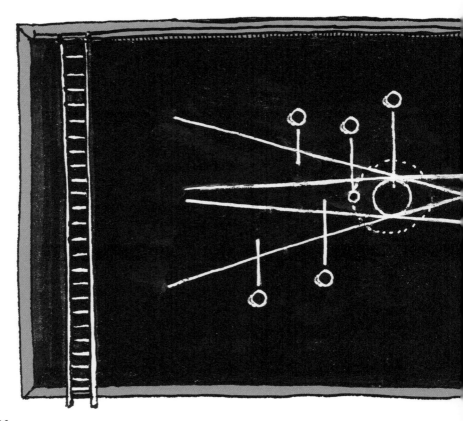

Born in 1768 into a well-educated family in Anhui province, Wang spent her childhood in the vast library of her grandfather, a former governor who owned more than 70 volumes of books. He introduced her to astronomy, while her father – a scholar who wrote books on medicine – taught her mathematics. Though most Chinese women at the time were cloistered at home and expected to remain quiet and docile – as one early Chinese saying went,

"a woman is virtuous only if she is untalented"[20] – Wang's family clearly saw the value in educating their bright and quick-witted daughter.

In turn, Wang had a knack for seeking out female mentors and teachers: when her well-travelled family moved to Jilin, in northeast China, the wife of a Mongol general taught her how to ride horses and shoot with a bow and arrow. When she turned 18, she met a group of female scholars in present-day Nanjing through their mutual love of poetry. At 25, she married and settled in Xuancheng in her home province, and began to build a name for herself as a poet and scientist.

"I have traveled ten thousand *li* and read ten thousand volumes," Wang once wrote.[21] Her extensive travels with her family had given her a thirst for knowledge and a keen eye for injustice: she wrote often of the poverty she had seen in the countryside and the inequality between the rich and the poor. Over her brief lifetime, she wrote enough poetry to fill 13 volumes.

Despite a head start, courtesy of her father and grandfather, Wang would sometimes struggle with her studies in mathematics and astronomy. "There were times that I had to put down the pen and sigh," she said. "But I love the subject, I do not give up."[22] However, it was her scientific achievements that truly distinguished her. At the time, most people in China did not understand the movement of the planets and how these affected lunar and solar eclipses, which were thought to be signs of the gods' anger. One of Wang's great successes was to explain accurately a lunar eclipse by way of her own scientific experiment: she built a model in a garden pavilion to demonstrate the movements of the celestial bodies, with a round table standing in for the earth, a mirror for the moon and a crystal lamp as the sun. By moving these around, she showed that a lunar eclipse is caused when the moon passes directly behind our planet and into its shadow.

Wang didn't stop there; she found ways to explain and calculate the equinoxes, analysed the movement of the planets and stars, and adopted an open-minded approach to knowledge. When Chinese scholars rejected the Western calendar, Wang – ever the astronomer – realized that it was based more precisely on the movement of the sun and rebuked her fellow scholars: "What counts is the usefulness, no matter whether it is Chinese or Western."[23]

Wang also saw the value in making scientific knowledge more accessible. She was quick to understand complex mathematical principles – including Pythagoras' theorem – and adept at translating them for a wider audience. With *The Musts of Calculation*, she rewrote the respected mathematician Mei Wending's unwieldy work into straightforward and simple language, and at 24 published her own five-volume text, *The Simple Principles of Calculation* (1792).

The cause of Wang's death remains unknown, but she knew that she was dying before she turned 30 and passed on her manuscripts to her best friend, instructing her to preserve them. It is thought that she authored six books on mathematics and astronomy, though none of them have survived. But her spirit lives on in the generations of scholars who came after her, and in her firm belief that men and women, as she put it, "are all people, who have the same reason for studying".[24]

n 22 January 1898, the moon slid between the earth and the sun, sending parts of central Africa and Asia into darkness. In India, **Annie Scott Dill Maunder** (1868–1947) was poised with an impressive camera she had retrofitted herself for the purpose of capturing the total solar eclipse. With a wide-angle lens 3.8cm (1½in) in diameter, she photographed an enormous ray-like structure appearing to burst from the sun: a coronal streamer, which we now understand to be charged particles attempting to break free from the fiery surface of the sun. According to calculations, the streamer was 10 million kilometres (6.2 million miles) in length: the biggest streamer ever captured on film. "As regards the corona," one astronomy writer later observed of Maunder's photograph, "Mrs Maunder with her tiny lens has beaten all the big instruments."[25]

Maunder was born Annie Scott Dill Russell in County Tyrone, Northern Ireland, to a Presbyterian minister and was the eldest of six children. After attending the most prestigious girls' school in Belfast, she bypassed Irish university in favour of the entrance exam to Girton College, one of the new women's colleges at Cambridge. Despite not having prepared for the open exam, 18-year-old Maunder did exceptionally well and earned a three-year scholarship.

"More than ordinarily handicapped – even for a woman – by an insufficiency of preliminary training, nothing but the power Miss Russell has of throwing herself completely into her work, could have enabled her to read as far as she has, and with such success,"[26] her mathematics tutor noted. He may not have been able to resist a little dig at her gender, but Maunder graduated as the top mathematician of her Girton cohort regardless.

In 1889 few scientific institutions were willing to employ women, even if said woman had graduated with honours in Cambridge's notoriously rigorous Mathematical Tripos. Fortunately, the Royal Observatory in Greenwich, London, was looking to hire a few supernumerary women computers. Much like their contemporaries at Harvard (see page 14), the women computers were expected to do menial mathematical work. Unlike at Harvard, however, these women also had the freedom to use the instruments and make their own observations. Maunder was earning £80 plus board a month as a teacher at a girls' school in Jersey, but applied for a job at the Observatory as soon as she heard of a vacancy.

She was offered a £4 monthly salary by the chief assistant to the Royal Astronomer, an amount so small that, in her own words, she "could scarcely live on it".[27]

Maunder was sent to work in the solar department, a unit tasked with observing the sun. Her boss was Edward Walter Maunder, a widower in his forties. Maunder's daily duties consisted of photographing sections of the sun, developing the film, then poring over the negatives to calculate the relative position of each sunspot. It was hoped that these tiny negatives would cumulatively assemble a better map of the only star in our solar system.

There was a 17-year age difference between Annie and Edward (known as Walter), but the stars aligned for them all the same. Though their marriage was a happy one, Annie was made to resign from the Observatory once she had tied the knot: it was considered inappropriate for a married woman to be engaged in full-time occupation. Thankfully, as noted by one Royal Astronomical

Society writer, "love on both sides was deep and true, and their aims and interests in life were the same."[28] Walter could no more force Annie to give up science than he could himself. When he founded the British Astronomical Association in 1890, Annie became the editor of its journal. But when she was proposed as a fellow of the Royal Astronomical Society in 1892, the other members turned up their noses at the admission of a woman and voted her down in a secret ballot.

Annie and Walter embarked on astronomical expeditions that took them to far-flung places, including Lapland and Algiers. It was on one of their trips to Asia that Annie captured her record-busting coronal streamer. In 1901, a visit to Mauritius to photograph another solar eclipse yielded yet another startling discovery. Annie's incredibly detailed images from the vantage point of the then-British colony showed key differences in the sun's corona when compared to other pictures taken by a team in Sumatra just one and a half hours earlier. It demonstrated that the sun's appearance waxes and wanes, just like the moon's.

Annie wasn't just taking photographs, either; every picture entailed complicated mathematical analysis to figure out exactly what she was looking at and how it related to her greater understanding of the sun. Based on decades of joint observation, the Maunders also discovered that the latitudes of sunspots vary cyclically over time, and are known for observing the Maunder Minimum: a period between 1645 and 1715 in which sunspots dwindled dramatically in number. Annie's name, however, was often subsumed under that of her husband's, a fact best exemplified by the joint byline on *The Heavens and Their Story* (1908), a popular science book that Walter admits in the introduction was "almost wholly the work of my wife".[29]

In 1916, the First World War prompted Maunder's return to the Royal Observatory, albeit as an unpaid volunteer, to make up for the wartime shortage in staff. That year, the Royal Astronomical Society relented and elected her a fellow at last on her husband's proposal. "Men learnt how the world on which they lived was set amongst the shining lights of heaven, and how these seemed to move around it," she wrote in *The Heavens and Their Story*. "They learned in time the shape and size of that world; then of the size and distance of moon and sun and planets. Then, greatly daring, they have soared upward to the stars, and tried to stretch the line of thought out to the uttermost depths of that unfathomable immensity."[30] Maunder's credit was to do the same as a woman.

n 1959, the Australian Security Intelligence Organisation had its eye on women's rights advocate, scientist and suspected communist **Ruby Payne-Scott** (1912–1981). An anonymous informant had filed a report on the go-getting Aussie, one of the first female physicists working at the Radiophysics Laboratory of the then Council for Scientific and Industrial Research (CSIR) in Sydney: "[Ruby] may be a supporter of [human rights activist] Jessie Street but it is not known whether that is in the political or feminist field," adding, "I would not put anything beyond her."[31] After all, this was the woman who had pretty much invented a new field of science with nothing but her own ingenuity, a few coat hangers and sticky tape.

Born in 1912 in Grafton, New South Wales, Payne-Scott won a scholarship to the University of Sydney at the age of 16, where she was the third ever female physics graduate in its history. Despite her honours in physics and mathematics, few companies or labs were willing to take on a female physicist at a time when physics wasn't even on the syllabus for most girls in her native New South Wales.

Payne-Scott had to scale back her ambition, studying for a teaching diploma and satisfying herself with a job at a South Australian school. But when Australia was thrust into the Second World War in 1939 – bringing with it a drought of scientific manpower as men signed up to fight – she sensed that her time had come. She applied to join the CSIR, which was looking to recruit 60 of Australia's brightest physicists to develop the country's emerging radar capabilities.

Radar was a hugely important part of Australia's defence against its Japanese enemies in the Pacific. To throw any spies off the scent, the radar development unit was titled the Radiophysics Laboratory. The work was so top secret that its lab was guarded by police officers, but wartime shortages meant that the equipment was often cobbled

together out of improvised materials. In Payne-Scott's hands, wire hangers and tape became crucial parts of wartime machinery to guard Australia's coastline. Over the course of the war, she became the leading expert in Australia on how to detect enemy aircraft using the radar display system known as the plan position indicator (PPI).

Payne-Scott and her colleague Joan Freeman were the only two women on the research team and they often had to navigate the sexist double standards of the time, which Payne-Scott did with her usual aplomb. When told that women were barred from wearing shorts in the workplace during summer, she pointed out that wearing a dress or a skirt to climb up ladders to reach the aerials was far more inappropriate. (A subsequent photo of Payne-Scott with her colleagues at CSIR shows her triumphantly attired in shorts.)

When the war came to an end, the Radiophysics Laboratory faced a conundrum: the crack team of physicists was now at a loose end. The CSIR decided to stake the future of the lab on a completely new and speculative field of science: radio astronomy.

From the 1930s onward, astronomers knew of a kind of cosmic static that came from the sun and other astronomical bodies, but nobody understood why it occurred, or why it interfered so much with radio reception. Payne-Scott was hired as a full-time research assistant; her team drove to wartime radar outposts to commandeer the old equipment. This time, instead of pointing it at Australia's enemies, they directed it at the sun.

They made some miraculous discoveries. At the time, scientists believed that the surface of the sun was almost 6,000°C (11,000°F). With her impeccable grasp of mathematics, Payne-Scott helped to work out that the sun's temperatures hit several million degrees. With her radar-honed eye, she also discovered different types of solar flares and the radio signals they emit as they erupt near the surface of the sun. Radio astronomy had scarcely received any attention at all; now the world turned to Australia as the leaders in explosive revelations about the universe.

But things weren't perfect. Payne-Scott had to fight her corner on several issues, including that of equal pay. During the war, she was paid the same as her male colleagues, but her salary was reduced by a third once back in her civvies. She argued her case so successfully that the Women's Employment Board even ended up giving her money to cover her losses for the time she was underpaid. Her outspokenness about equal pay and her trade union activities soon caught the eye of the Australian secret service. As it turns out, Payne-Scott was indeed a card-carrying Communist Party member, but government spies were never able to find any firm evidence.

Payne-Scott was eventually forced out of science, not because of her politics, but because of her marriage. Under Commonwealth law, a woman had to resign from her permanent position in the Australian Public Service on the day she was married. All through her years as Australia's pioneering radio astronomer, Payne-Scott had been hiding a secret: she had married a man called William Holman Hall in 1944. She was finally exposed in 1950 and fought her CSIR managers to stay. In one blistering letter, she declared her opinion of the unjust law: "Personally I feel no legal or moral obligation to have taken any other action than I have in making my marriage known...The present procedure is ridiculous and can lead to ridiculous results."[32]

It was a battle she couldn't win and she was eventually made to resign by those in charge at CSIR. At her farewell party, her boss described her as the best physicist in the lab. She never returned to science; she took a job as the mathematics and science teacher at a girls' school in Sydney. There, as one student put it, "The staff and students at Danebank had no idea of the brilliant career that Mrs Ruby Hall had led."[33]

Biology &
natural sciences

uring the 18th and 19th centuries in Britain, it wasn't unusual to spot locals and tourists hunting for dinosaur fossils on the beaches of the seaside village of Lyme Regis in Dorset. Its vertiginous coastal cliffs brimmed with long-dead creatures, their skeletons packed into the thin layers of shale and limestone. The fossils were destined to be sold off to private collectors, academics and museums at eye-watering prices. There was plenty of competition among those who sought their fortune and fame in the study of ancient bones, but only one woman had an unerring eye for the art of fossil hunting: **Mary Anning** (1799–1847), the "princess of paleontology."[1]

Born in 1799 into a working-class family of furniture makers, Anning clearly had luck on her side from a very young age. As a 14-month-old baby, she survived a lightning strike that claimed the lives of three others. Her father, Richard, sold fossils to supplement his income as a carpenter, and had taught Anning and her brother the ins and outs of hunting for these so-called "curiosities".[2] But disaster struck when Anning was ten years old: Richard fell off a cliff en route to the nearby village of Charmouth and, in his weakened state, passed away after contracting tuberculosis.

Richard was Anning's earliest mentor, but he was not a particularly fiscally responsible father. He left behind debts of £120 – a huge amount at the time – which almost pushed the Anning family into poverty, forcing them to rely on parish relief for the poor. Mary continued chipping away at the cliffs and searching for bones. One day, she ran into a woman on the street, who spotted a small ammonite fossil in the young girl's hand and offered her half a crown for it.

This chance sale changed the course of Anning's life. A couple of years later, her brother spotted part of an *Ichthyosaurus* fossil in the mudslide-prone cliff of Black Ven. Almost a year later, she excavated the rest of the skeleton and sold it all to a rich local collector for £23. Over the next decade, the Annings

set about establishing their fossil shop in town. Though Anning was already more adept at fossil-finding than her brother, the endeavour was sometimes hit and miss. When the family went almost a year without discovering anything, a philanthropic collector was so moved by their plight that he sold off his fossils to help them avoid financial ruin.

By 1825, Anning had taken over the shop from her mother and her brother had left to become a furniture upholsterer. With her fossil-hunting hammer in hand and her trusty terrier Tray by her side, she braved the hanging cliffs in search of bones every day. Winter brought the threat of rain and landslides, and she narrowly avoided being crushed by one in 1833. (Her dog was not so lucky.)

Anning was only 24 when she discovered the first completely intact specimen of *Plesiosaurus*, a marine dinosaur with the head of a lizard and the large, paddle-like fins of a whale. Its announcement drew the biggest audience on record for the Geological Society in London and Anning became a sensation in the relatively young field of palaeontology. Upper-class ladies and gentlemen travelled from London to Lyme to meet this provincial fossil-hunting wunderkind. Anning would graciously receive visitors in her small shop, surrounded by hundreds of specimens, and impress them with her knowledge of anatomy and science. Anning's finds even inspired artwork; when she discovered the first pterosaur skeleton in Britain, it prompted one artist to paint the winged dinosaur in flight above the storm-tossed beaches of Lyme.

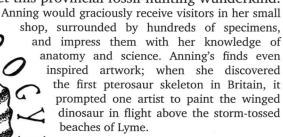

One well-heeled visitor wrote of Anning:

"It is certainly a wonderful instance of divine favour that this poor, ignorant girl should be so blessed, for by reading and application she has arrived to that degree of knowledge as to be in the habit of writing and talking with professors and other clever men on the subject, and they all acknowledge that she understands more of the science than anyone else in this kingdom."[3]

Unfortunately, public success did not mean scientific recognition. Though she was a skilled scientific illustrator and nimbly sketched many of her skeletons, she had published nothing in her own name. Because of her class, background and gender, she was never quite regarded by her peers as a palaeontologist, though she knew far more about fossils than the men who flocked to buy them from her. By the time she died at the age of 47, Anning had excavated five major specimens – including *Squaloraja*, a fossil fish that suggested an evolutionary link between sharks and rays – but her role in discovering these creatures was essentially erased. In museums and public galleries, the honour of discovery didn't go to the actual discoverer; it went to the rich gentleman who bought and donated the specimen. This is slowly changing: in the Natural History Museum, London, you can spot Anning's large-skulled plesiosaur in the marine reptile collection. If you look hard, just as Anning did, you can spot her footprints all over the history of palaeontology.

 spidery worm crawls over the sunshine-yellow skin of a ripe pomelo fruit, witnessed from above by a fully grown green-banded urania moth with golden wings;[4] a papery cocoon hangs off a frangipani plant in bloom as an adult red cracker butterfly perches on its stalk.[5] More than three centuries after **Maria Sibylla Merian** (1647–1717) committed the image of these insects to paper, they retain their vivid, almost hallucinogenic appeal. They are also meticulously observed and scientifically accurate; after all, the German naturalist was a perfectionist who, dissatisfied with drawing from preserved specimens, got on a boat all the way to the other side of the world to get a better view.

Today, Merian is thought to be one of the greatest scientific illustrators of all time. She was born in 1647 in Frankfurt, Germany. Her stepfather was a still-life painter who taught her illustration and encouraged her love of nature. At 13, she became entranced by insects, especially the way that caterpillars transformed into butterflies and moths. She reared silkworms at home, feeding them with lettuce and mulberries, to better paint and observe their metamorphosis.

Even after she married Johann Andreas Graff, a painter and engraver, and bore two daughters, she wandered the countryside and public gardens looking for insects to catch. However, Merian wasn't just looking for specimens to take home and paint: instead she would carefully take note of their behaviour, feeding pattern and the various stages of their metamorphosis.

In 1679, she published her first scientific work: *Der Raupen wunderbare Verwandelung und sonderbare Blumen-nahrung* ("The wondrous transformation of caterpillars and their remarkable diet of flowers"). In her distinctive illustrations, the entire life cycle of the insect is depicted on its host plant. Merian's book was one of the first to show insects from larva to adult and their relationship to the plant kingdom, and she quickly followed it with another volume of illustration four years later.

During this time, Merian's marriage fell apart. Along with her two daughters and mother, she took the drastic step of moving into a Dutch religious commune where her half-brother already lived. This taste of freedom clearly suited her; Graff tried and failed to win her back, and in 1791 she left the sect and settled in Amsterdam, a newly divorced woman.

The capital of the Dutch empire was heaving with trade and business. But Merian wasn't interested in the spices or riches from the colonies; she was transfixed by their insects. The collections of merchants and missionaries were teeming with outlandish tropical specimens she had never seen before, but there was one problem: they were all dead. Merian wanted to paint these insects alive.

At the age of 52, Merian drew up her will and set sail with her younger daughter for the South American colony of Dutch Surinam. People thought the trip was ridiculous; an old woman embarking on a perilous trip for the sake of scientific inquiry was unheard of. When she made it to Surinam, she spent two years engrossed in her study of its flora and fauna. Merian roamed plantations, river banks, gardens and jungles to collect insect specimens and their host plant, transporting hundreds to her temporary residence and painting them as they progressed from caterpillar to butterfly. In total, she observed and painted more than 90 animal species and around 60 different plant species.

After a serious illness forced her to return to Amsterdam, in 1705 Merian was persuaded by some amateur naturalists to publish her paintings in a book. The result – a magnum opus of 60 plates titled *Metamorphosis insectorum Surinamensium* ("Transformation of the Surinamese insects") – astounded scientists and art collectors alike. Many of these exotic and unknown animals had never been documented before in such detail.

To this day, Merian is believed to be one of the only people to have recorded the life cycles of some insect species, and many of her scientific observations about their behaviour and metamorphosis are still accurate. Her book influenced scores of naturalists for generations to come and set the standard for scientific illustration for decades. But for all her gutsiness, Merian remained humble about her art:

"In making this work I did not seek to profit myself; rather, I was content merely to cover my costs; I spared no expense in executing this work; I had the plates engraved by the most renowned masters, and used the best paper in order to please both the connoisseurs of art and the amateur naturalists interested in insects and plants. It will also give me great pleasure to hear that I have achieved my aim at the same time as giving people pleasure."[6]

In that respect, she certainly succeeded.

n 1967 **Dian Fossey** (1932–1985) travelled to the tangled forests of Mount Bisoke in Rwanda to begin her study of mountain gorillas. At the time, many people believed that these great apes were savage and ferocious beasts. Fossey – a primatologist with little formal training, but with an intense love of animals – devoted her life to dispelling this myth. It was a calling that would ultimately end in her brutal murder at the age of 53.

Fossey wrote in her 1970 *National Geographic* despatch, the first of many articles she would write for the publication:

"For the past three years I have spent most of my days with wild mountain gorillas. Their home, and mine, has been the misty wooded slopes of the Virunga range, eight lofty volcanoes – the highest is 14,787 feet – shared by three African nations, Rwanda, Uganda, and the Democratic Republic of the Congo."[7]

Fossey did not set out to become one of the world's foremost primate researchers. As a young woman, she pursued occupational therapy after dropping out of her veterinary science course. But when a once-in-a-lifetime trip to Africa resulted in a chance encounter with leading paleoanthropologist Louis Leakey, Fossey gave up her life in Louisville, Kentucky, to move to an East African mountain range some 12,000 kilometres (7,600 miles) away.

The aim? To study one of only two populations of mountain gorillas existing in the wild. Leakey was convinced that scientists needed to study humanity's closest ancestors to gain a better understanding of evolution. He had already persuaded primatologist Jane Gooddall to research chimpanzees; now he was looking for someone to take on gorillas.

What Fossey discovered was revelatory. "The gorilla is one of the most maligned animals in the world," she wrote. "After more than 2,000 hours of direct observation, I can account for less than five minutes of what might be called 'aggressive' behaviour."[8]

Fossey was one of the first to realize that it wasn't enough to simply silently observe these gentle, shy animals. To get close to the gorillas, she'd have to win their trust and that meant behaving like them. "The gorillas have responded favorably, although admittedly these methods are not always dignified," she wrote. "One feels a fool thumping one's chest rhythmically, or sitting about pretending to munch on a stalk of wild celery as though it were the most delectable morsel in the world."[9]

Her unique approach worked wonders. Fossey was soon accepted by the group and was able to observe their diet, social behaviour and mating patterns in greater detail than ever before.

But she was also keenly aware that she was up against the clock: the mountain gorilla was predicted to become extinct in two or three decades. In the 1960s there were fewer than 500 in the Virunga Mountains alone.

The photographs and video footage that emerged out of Rwanda, courtesy of Fossey, changed the way the world looked at gorillas and brought no end of publicity and conservation funds. With her *National Geographic* coverage and subsequent memoirs, *Gorillas in the Mist* (1983), she went from being a research pioneer to an international sensation. But Fossey was also a deeply divisive and alienating figure. As she grew older, she became increasingly obsessed with fighting the poachers who threatened the gorillas.

She called this "active conservation"; in practice, it meant terrorizing poachers and hunters alike with guard patrols, physical abuse and threats of black magic. "We stripped him and spread-eagled him outside my cabin and lashed the holy blue sweat out of him with nettle stalks,"[10] Fossey recalled in one letter.

Fossey unravelled even further after the death of her favourite gorilla, Digit. In 1977, the 12-year-old animal was found dead; his head and hands had been hacked off by poachers. A heartbroken Fossey began smoking and drinking heavily, and she grew increasingly contemptuous and hateful toward the locals. She abandoned her research, alienating fellow researchers and focusing on her aggressive anti-poaching tactics. Fossey was accused of embodying the worst colonial and racist attitudes toward Rwandans, and even she seemed to acknowledge her own bitterness. "I have no friends," she said. "The more that you learn about the dignity of the gorilla, the more you want to avoid people."[11]

On Boxing Day in 1985, she was murdered in her cabin and the case was never solved. To some former colleagues, her death came as no surprise; Fossey had made many enemies over the years. But she also laid the foundations for a global conservation movement and assured the survival of her beloved animals. Today, the mountain gorilla remains critically endangered, but their numbers are slowly growing and researchers in Rwanda continue to monitor and observe the descendants of the gorillas that Fossey loved so much.

hen the UN Charter was signed by members of the fledgling United Nations in 1945, there were only four female delegates – out of a total of 850 – there to sign it. **Bertha Lutz** (1894–1976), a Brazilian zoologist, was one of them, and she believed that the foundational treaty of the UN was lacking something: women.

In fact, the word "women" wasn't mentioned once in the draft of the UN founding treaty. This meant that half of the world had been effectively omitted from its greatest peacekeeping and human rights organization. With the support of a group of female representatives from Latin America and Australia, Lutz fought successfully for the inclusion of women so that the Charter affirmed "the dignity and worth of the human person, in the equal rights of men and women."[12]

Her efforts weren't exactly appreciated by her colleagues in the West. US delegate Virginia Gildersleeve confronted Lutz and told her "not to ask for anything for women in the Charter since that would be a very vulgar thing to do."[13] British representative Ellen Wilkinson told Lutz that gender equality already existed because she had just been appointed to the King's Privy Council. "I'm afraid not," Lutz recalls informing her, "it only means that you have arrived."[14]

Lutz was born in 1894 to an English nurse and a Swiss-Brazilian naturalist and physician in São Paulo. Her father specialized in tropical medicine and Lutz often followed him on rainforest expeditions to collect specimens of her favourite animal: tree frogs, or as she called them, "my brothers the frogs."[15] While studying for a degree in biology at the Sorbonne in Paris, Lutz developed an interest in the growing women's suffrage movement in the UK. She didn't agree with the violence used by British suffragettes, but she felt a keen affinity with their goals.

When Lutz returned home in 1918, she was incensed by a newspaper columnist's declaration that the recent feminist achievements in the UK and the US would have no effect on

Brazil. She issued a passionate call for a political league of Brazilian women who believed that women should contribute to society in all areas of life, including politics and business. Brazilian society thought that women were best confined to the domestic sphere, though Lutz found sly ways of arguing around this: "Women's domain, all feminists agree, is the home," she said of female participation in politics. "But...nowadays the home no longer is just the space encompassed within four walls."[16]

In 1922 she followed her own advice and founded the Federação Brasileira pelo Progresso Feminino (FBPF), or Brazilian Federation for the Advancement of Women. Its initial success was modest and reflected the concerns of its educated, upper-middle-class membership. For example, it successfully lobbied the government to allow girls to attend its most prestigious academy, Colégio Pedro II, an elite breeding ground for future politicians and movers and shakers.

Lutz didn't neglect her love of herpetology (the study of amphibians and reptiles); in fact, she sometimes found novel ways to combine the two interests. When she travelled to Baltimore, Maryland, in 1922 to attend the first Pan-American Conference of Women, a groundbreaking political summit that gathered together women from 32 countries, she astonished a delegate by sinking to her knees near a stream and pulling a frog from the water. Examining her prize catch, she explained that it was the first time she had ever seen such a specimen, and spent the rest of the day collecting more for her lab. Even as she fought tirelessly for women's rights, she continued to research and publish scientific studies on her favourite amphibians, and even discovered a new species of frog, which now bears the name Lutz's rapids frog.

Lutz knew the importance of guaranteeing the legal rights of women. She studied for a law degree in Rio de Janeiro, and in 1932 she led a FBPF delegation to meet with Brazilian president Getúlio Vargas, to argue for women's suffrage as his government prepared to rewrite the country's electoral code. When women finally went to the polls in 1933, Brazil officially became the sixth country in the world to grant women the vote. Lutz was appointed to the commission in charge of rewriting the country's constitution and she made sure that it incorporated women's rights, including the right to earn equal pay and hold public office. (She even ran for government herself, but failed to win a seat.)

Even after Vargas seized power in 1937 and shut down Congress, Lutz continued to represent Brazil at international conferences, including that fateful United Nations conference in 1945. She remained proud that it was the women of her region who were pushing for equality. "The mantle is falling off the shoulders of the Anglo-Saxons," she wrote in her memoirs. "We [Latin American women] shall have to do the next stage of battle for women."[17]

hen **Jane Colden's** (1724–1766) father taught her botany, he probably never guessed she would go down in history as America's first female botanist. After all, Cadwallader Colden had sailed to the New World to seek his fortune in New York after training as a doctor at the University of Edinburgh, and he had brought Scotland's 18th-century attitudes toward women with him, writing to a botanist friend in Holland:

"I (often) thought that Botany is an amusement which may be made greater to the Ladies who are often at a loss to fill up their time (& that) it could be made agreeable to them (it would prevent their employing so much of their time in trifling amusements as they do)."[18]

Whatever Jane made of her father's reasons for educating her, she took to the study of plants with a passion and verve that clearly impressed him. "She has now grown very fond of the study, and has made such progress in it that as I believe would please you if you saw her performance," Cadwallader continued in his letter. For a man who fancied himself something of a natural scientist and regularly corresponded with some of Europe's leading botanists, there could be no higher praise.

Jane Colden was born in 1724 in Orange County, New York, on a vast 1,200-hectare (3,000-acre) estate that her family named Coldengham. New York state was a newly established British colony that had been wrestled from the Dutch some six decades previously, and Coldengham was an especially wild corner of land, full of obscure and curious plants that the Coldens had never encountered in Scotland. Jane inherited the scientific curiosity of her father, who made a special effort to train his promising daughter in Swedish naturalist Carl Linnaeus's recently developed taxonomic system, a then-revolutionary way to classify flora and fauna.

By 1757 Colden had finished an exhaustive investigation of the plant life of the region, describing and classifying no less than 340 native specimens in a notebook that also featured illustrations and sketches. Other New Yorkers would visit Coldengham bearing interesting seeds and other plants for Colden's perusal. Her abilities didn't just extend to examining and recording the physical attributes of each specimen and its various iterations from seed to flower and fruit; she also spoke to Native American people of the area, to note the plant's potential medicinal qualities right down to its dosage and preparation, and cross-referencing this with other physicians.

Of *Asclepias tuberosa*, a species of milkweed now known as butterfly weed, she wrote:

"The Root of this Asclepias taken in powder, is an excellent cure for the Colick, about halff a Spoonfull at a time. This cure was learn'd from a Canada Indian, & is calld in New England Canada Root. The Exellency of this Root for the Colik is confirmed by Dr. Porter of New England, and Dr. Brooks of Maryland likewise confirm'd this. One ounce of the Root, chiped into small pieces, to which put a pint & a half of boiling water, & let it stew for about one hour, of this Decoction drinck halff a Tea cup full, every hour or two, and you bin certainly perfectly cured from the bloody Flux, and better is when you boil the Root in Claret than in Water. This cure was learnd from the Indians."[19]

Colden was no shrinking violet when it came to her own powers of observation, either. Though she was meticulous about keeping to the Linnaean classification system, she wasn't afraid to dispute the scientist's own judgments about plants. In one description of a plant known as snakeroot, she wrote, "Linnaeus describes this as being a Papilionatious Flower...I must beg Leave to differ from him...the Seed Vessell, differs from all that I have observed of the Papilionatious Kind."[20]

In Colden's modest notebook lay the most comprehensive portrait ever made of New York's abundant vegetation. Her rigorous research and painstakingly detailed descriptions won the praise of her scientific contemporaries in both the New and the Old World, many of whom expressed amazement that a woman was capable of such scientific inquiry. London horticulturalist Peter Collinson even wrote to Linnaeus himself to recommend the "scientifically skilful" Colden to the founding father of botany: "[Caldwallader's] daughter is perhaps the first lady that has so perfectly studied your system. She deserves to be celebrated."[21]

Colden might have been a pioneer in the field of American botany, but her abilities were never able to take flight beyond the boundaries of the Coldengham estate. After marrying in 1759, it appears that she gave up botany altogether before dying seven years later at the age of 42. Today, Colden's manuscript lies in the natural history archive of the British Museum, London – the only scientific work she produced.

sther Lederberg (1922–2006) devoted her life to the study of small and invisible organisms: bacteria, to be precise. But while some of her work has gone unrecognized and uncredited, her contribution to science was anything but minuscule.

When Stanford microbiologist Stanley Falkow was introduced to Lederberg in 1960, she was deep in conversation with a lab colleague and peering intently at a petri dish of typhoid bacteria. "Her glasses were perched on her forehead and she held the plate of bacteria so close to her face that I feared her nose would touch the colonies," he said at her memorial service.

Born during the Great Depression in New York – when lunch at the Lederbergs' often consisted of a tomato squeezed onto a slice of bread – Esther was advised to study French and literature at college. Instead, she opted for biochemistry. As an impoverished student, she washed her landlady's clothes to pay rent and ate the frogs' legs from student dissections. Her diligence paid off and she received her master's degree in genetics from Stanford in 1946.

Later that year, she and her husband, the molecular biologist Joshua Lederberg, relocated to the University of Wisconsin. It was there that Esther made some of the biggest discoveries in microbiology, such as lambda phage, a type of virus that lives in a strain of *E. coli* bacteria. This tiny organism revolutionized the emerging field of molecular genetics. Unlike others in its family, the virus doesn't replicate and destroy its host. It is able to reside peacefully

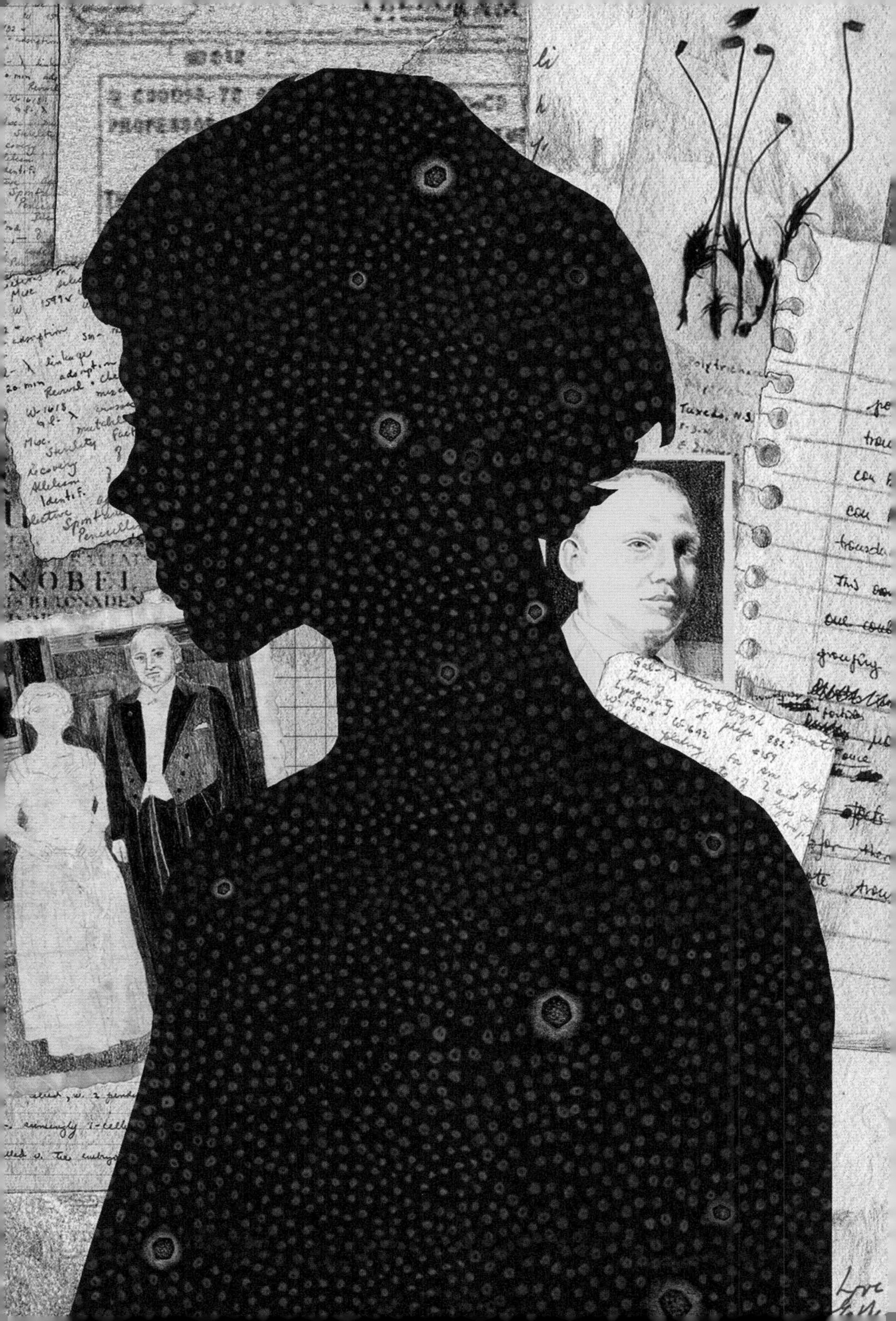
NOBEL

within *E. coli* without appearing to harm the cell; the *E. coli* then divides normally into a new cell, albeit one that has inherited the DNA of lambda phage. That made it a perfect candidate for scientists seeking to better understand the regulation and transmission of genes.

In 1952 Esther was instrumental in developing another breakthrough technique. By then, she and Joshua were working as a team and were investigating how bacteria become resistant to drugs. The early process of transferring colonies of bacteria was time-consuming and inefficient, but Esther theorized that the fibres in a regular piece of shop-bought velvet could act like minuscule needles and transfer bacteria onto a new plate. By pressing the scrap of cloth onto a colonized petri dish and stamping it onto a fresh plate, bacteria could be reproduced with a minimum of fuss.

With a few spare dollars and a scrap of sterilized velveteen, the Lederbergs pioneered the replica plating process. Thanks to their new technique, they found that spontaneous mutations arise in bacteria, allowing them to become resistant to drugs such as penicillin. Improved versions of replica plating are still used in labs all over the world.

It was work such as this that contributed to Joshua winning the Nobel Prize in Physiology or Medicine in 1958. Esther, however, did not share in the Prize. Many now believe that the work that led to the award could not have happened without her contributions, though she brushed off the exclusion. "One must stop thinking about the Nobel Laureates as having the last word," she remarked in a 1985 interview. "They are chosen by a committee that sits in Stockholm. I don't take it very seriously."[22]

Esther and Joshua divorced in 1966 after moving back to Stanford. According to her second husband, Matthew Simon, Stanford was less keen on the idea of the solo female scientist now that she had split from her husband and no longer worked in partnership with him. Esther had to fight for her position and was allowed in only as an untenured professor. She would never achieve tenure while at Stanford, though she did found the Plasmid Reference Center in 1976: a global toolkit and archive of small DNA molecules that hold the key to vital traits such as antibiotic resistance, which scientists continue to draw from today.

By the time of her death at the age of 83, Lederberg's pioneering techniques were common in microbiology labs everywhere; she even discovered a new virus that scientists had never identified before. But she was always humble about the nature and scope of her work: "Scientific research can only work with tools and substances. If it can't be approached that way then science can say nothing about it," she once said. "You have to be neutral or open. That is the only thing you can do. We only go as far as our tools go."[23]

*i*f you have ever felt adrift in life or worried that you're on the wrong track, then think of **Ynés Mexía** (1870–1938), a Mexican-American botanist who discovered her true calling at 51 and would go on to discover 500 new plant species and become one of the greatest collectors of her generation.

Mexía was plagued by bad luck in her early adult life. She was born in Washington DC to an American mother and a Mexican diplomat father; her parents split up when she was a child. She hopped between schools in Philadelphia, Ontario and Maryland, before ending up at her father's hacienda in Mexico. Disaster struck when her first husband died in 1898, and her second marriage, to a man 16 years her junior, nearly bankrupted her and destroyed the successful business she had built. She left Mexico City in 1908 for San Francisco, which she would call home for the rest of her life.

Mexía divorced her second husband on her return to the US, but struggled with depression in the wake of the separation. Then she found something in San Francisco that made her feel better: plants. In 1917, the environmental organisation the Sierra Club was already a quarter of a century old and drawing nature lovers from all over the country. In her days off from her job as a social worker, Mexía signed up to her local chapter, joining them on hikes through the countryside and throwing herself into a campaign to save the Californian redwoods. She was 51 when she decided to enrol as a mature student at the University of California at Berkeley to learn more about natural science.

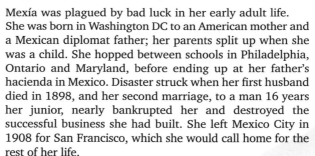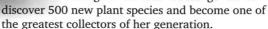

Berkeley introduced Mexía to what would become her greatest passion: botanical collecting. At the beginning of the 20th century, vast numbers of plant species were still unknown to Western audiences; intrepid botanical adventurers would travel to far-flung places to bring back specimens for scientific study. In 1925 Mexía joined their ranks and set off for Sinaloa, Mexico, on a Stanford University-sponsored expedition. As she admitted in a letter to a friend, "I am not a dyed-in-the-wool scientist, I am a nature lover and a bit of an adventuress."[24] These journeys were not without danger; on one occasion, Mexía fractured her ribs after falling off a cliff.

Early on in the trip, however, Mexía realized that she was more of a solo explorer. She left her group behind, commandeered her own supplies and travelled to Mazatlan by herself. She ended up staying in Mexico for two more years and collected more than 3,500 specimens, which she dutifully posted back to the herbarium in Berkeley. Among the plants were 50 species that had never been recorded before, including one new genus of flowering plant, which was named *Mexianthus mexicus* in honour of the woman who first spotted it.

The fruitful Mexico trip marked the beginning of 13 years of nonstop travel and discovery. Mexía's collecting adventures would take her to Brazil, Peru, Ecuador, back to Mexico and home to the US to document the unique flora of Alaska. In 1929 she canoed along the Amazon, tracing it all the way

to its source in the Andes mountains some 4,800 kilometres (3,000 miles) upstream.

In the Amazon, Mexía gave sewing needles and fish hooks to the indigenous tribes that greeted her and her guides, and camped out on sandy riverbanks stalked by jaguars and tapirs. She even survived a vicious whirlpool, which almost sucked her raft in before spitting it out. "Up at dawn," she wrote cheerfully of her daily routine, as she advanced farther and farther into the depths of the rainforest, "and another day of inching the heavy canoe past monstrous stranded trees...At last the long-desired wilderness, untouched and unmarred by the hand of man."[25]

It was on an expedition in Oaxaca, Mexico, that Mexía fell ill. She died a few years later in 1938, having collected more than 145,000 specimens in total and with more than 50 species named in her honour. But it was the thrill of adventure that drove this unlikely explorer. As she wrote in her travelogue on arriving in Ecuador:

"The Land of the Equator! There my life-long shadow would dog my step no longer, but, vanquished, would grovel beneath my feet. At last I would stand on the earth's great belt, nearest the beneficent sun. But would it be beneficent, or would it strike me down with its invisible power or burn me with its intense rays?"[26]

For Mexía, botany was more than just the collecting and indexing of plants: it was the promise of conquering new horizons and, in the process, her own limitations.

rowing up in the lush foothills of Kenya's central highlands, **Wangari Maathai** (1940–2011) would often fetch water for her mother from a stream that ran by their house. She drank straight from the brook, trying to pick up the frogspawn that lay on the surface of the water and watching the tadpoles wiggle their way out.

"This is the world I inherited from my parents," Maathai told the Nobel committee as she accepted the Peace Prize in 2004. "The challenge is to restore the home of the tadpoles and give back to our children a world of beauty and wonder."[27] When she saw the slow destruction of the Kenyan environment – including the drying up of her childhood stream – she dreamed of reforesting the country. By the time she passed away at the age of 71, Maathai had single-handedly led a campaign to plant 30 million trees in Africa as the founder of the Green Belt Movement.

Maathai was a bright child and won a scholarship abroad as part of the famous Kennedy Airlift, which saw hundreds of East Africans leave to study at US universities. After majoring in biology, she studied for a master's degree at the University of Pittsburgh, where she was impressed by the city's effort to clean up its air. It was her first brush with environmental restoration. That, and the energy of the university's anti-Vietnam War movement, left a lasting impression on Maathai.

She returned home in 1966 to study for a Ph.D in veterinary anatomy, becoming the first woman in East and Central Africa to gain a doctorate and the first to chair the University of Nairobi vet department. While travelling for work, Maathai saw how deforestation led to drought and poverty. When forests were cleared for commercial plantations, local biodiversity was reduced, food crops were diminished and water sources dried up. Women were on the frontlines of this struggle; they were the ones who had to walk for hours to find firewood and clean water.

Maathai's solution was simple: trees, and lots of them. The Green Belt Movement paid rural women a stipend to plant tree nurseries, encouraging them to protect the land and become self-sufficient. The act of planting a tree was small but revolutionary: the nurseries preserved rainwater, provided food and kindling, and put many women on the first step to financial independence. The Movement eventually grew to include more than 900,000 people and led to the planting of millions of trees.

In 1977 Maathai's husband filed for divorce, arguing that she was too stubborn and assertive. When she criticized the judge who granted the annulment, she was thrown in prison for contempt of court. "I should have known that ambition and success were not to be expected in an African woman,"

she said. "An African woman should be a good African woman whose qualities should be coyness, shyness, submissiveness, incompetence and crippling dependency. A highly educated independent African woman is bound to be dominant, aggressive, uncontrollable, a bad influence."[28] She never married again.

As the Green Belt Movement flourished, its democratic mission of environmental preservation locked horns with the increasingly authoritarian Kenyan government. President Daniel arap Moi labelled the Movement as "subversive" when Maathai criticized his construction plans for a 60-storey skyscraper in a Nairobi park.[29] She took him to court and the resulting international attention scared off Moi's foreign investors. Shortly afterward, Maathai's name was found on a government assassination list and she was arrested on charges of treason with sedition.

Maathai refused to back down. She even went on a hunger strike in the park to call for the release of other political prisoners and was described by Moi as "a threat to the order and security of the country".[30] A police beating left her in hospital, but she continued to speak out against the government even as she remained afraid for her life

In the 1990s, Maathai joined politics and set up Mazingira, a green political party, and went on to win a seat in parliament as part of the 2002 coalition that removed Moi's party. She served as a junior environment minister and was the winner of the Nobel Peace Prize two years later. In its remarks, the committee praised "her contribution to sustainable development, democracy and peace".[31]

Today, the Green Belt Movement has branches in 30 countries. Thanks to a Kenyan village girl turned scientist and environmental activist, the world is a greener and richer place. As she put it: "The tree is just a symbol for what happens to the environment. The act of planting one is a symbol of revitalizing the community. Tree planting is only the entry point into the wider debate about the environment. Everyone should plant a tree."[32]

Medicine &
psychology

ere's a little dirty joke from Martial, a wit and poet who lived in ancient Rome: "The young wife of an old man claims that she is suffering from hysteria and needs the standard regimen – that is, intercourse. And so, *protinus accedunt medici medicaeque recedunt* ('the male doctors arrive and the female doctors depart')."[1]

OK, so the punchline probably sounded better in the second century. But Martial's gag also highlights a lesser-known part of ancient Greco-Roman history: the existence of women in the medical profession. At a time when the vast majority of Greek women were confined to their homes – their greatest responsibilities consisting of running the household and bearing children – some managed to buck the trend by finding work as midwives, doctors and surgeons. One of them, **Aspasia** (*c*.4th century AD), pioneered surgical techniques that resemble those we use today, becoming one of the most respected and well-known gynaecologists of her age.

Little is known about Aspasia's personal life or training. There weren't any medical schools in ancient Greece and many doctors either came from a family of health practitioners or apprenticed under a more established mentor. There are also records of women doctors receiving training from their husbands. It is likely that Aspasia acquired her training through one of these routes, though she appears to have quickly surpassed the skills of her teacher.

Her original writing has been lost over time, but some of her teachings have been preserved in the works of her successors. The Byzantine physician and writer Aëtius of Amida repeatedly references Aspasia as a medical authority in *Tetrabiblos*, a mammoth health encyclopedia that contains an entire volume dedicated to gynaecology and women's health.

Through these records, Aspasia emerges as one of the earliest pioneers of obstetrics and gynaecology. She was sexual health clinic, medical surgery and family planning centre all rolled into one; Aspasia performed abortions, advised pregnant women and even removed uterine haemorrhoids.

In fact, she was far more progressive on contraception than some doctors and politicians today: she advocated abortion if her patient's life was at risk or if she had a pre-existing medical condition that made pregnancy unwise. Aspasia's methods of medical abortion included a herbal bath of abortifacient drugs such as fenugreek, marsh mallow and *Artemisia*; a suppository of salve made from the opopanax plant followed by a vaginal steam bath of female hair and burned garlic; or a boiled concoction of *Cyperus* leaves applied to the abdomen overnight.

Today, some of Aspasia's remedies might sound unusual, strange or just plain bizarre: steaming your vagina with garlic is unlikely to achieve anything, let alone induce an abortion. But much of her advice still makes sense today. To ensure a healthy pregnancy, Aspasia told pregnant patients to avoid stress, not lift heavy objects and keep away from spicy dishes or food that is hard to digest: all sensible tips that are dispensed by doctors today. (She also recommends women to steer clear of chariot rides on bumpy roads, which is somewhat less relevant in the 21st century.) Her guidance extended beyond preventative care, too: she pioneered a successful technique to rotate a breech foetus facing the wrong direction for birth.

Her knowledge didn't just encompass contraception and midwifery; she also developed new surgical methods to treat common reproductive health problems that both women and men experienced. In fact, many of the procedures she introduced continued to be used for centuries later.

When women developed bleeding or prolapsed uterine haemorrhoids (commonly known as fibroids), Aspasia correctly assessed that surgery was necessary to fix the problem. She advised that the haemorrhoids be "circularly incised around their basis and enfolded tightly with a loop",[2] a method of surgical excision that was practised until relatively recently.

The do-it-all doctor also invented a treatment to remove a hydrocele: a lump around a testicle that builds up as a result of excess fluid. "The incision should be linear, symmetrical to the lump," she instructs.

"After dividing the superficial skin and splitting the subjacent tissues, we cut through the integument which contains the fluid via a seared surgical clasp. When the fluid is depleted, we etch a circular demarcation and remove the pus in order to finally pass two or three sutures through the lips of the incision."[3]

This is startlingly similar to a modern-day hydrocelectomy, an operation in which the thin membrane that surrounds the testicles is cut open to drain the fluid.

Aspasia's innovative surgery skills and genuinely forward-looking approach to family planning should have guaranteed her a place in the hall of medical history; she certainly impressed many of her peers as well as later scholars. Unfortunately, like many women in antiquity, Aspasia is now only known to historians, though her legacy lives on in the field of gynaecology and obstetrics, which is today made up of 85 per cent women.[4]

hen **Fe del Mundo** (1911–2011) arrived at Harvard Medical School in 1936, her professors were dumbfounded. It wasn't because they forgot the doctor, who was on a presidential scholarship, was coming: they just didn't expect her to be a woman.

Nobody at one of America's most prestigious med schools had realized that Fe – whose full name means "faith of the world" in Spanish – was a woman's name. Harvard had never accepted a woman on to its course before. In 1878, in fact, it had turned down a $10,000 donation because the offer was linked to women's admission.[5] Now, some 54 years later, the school was faced with a quandary: Should Del Mundo be let in?

The faculty decided that the answer was yes. After all, she'd spent months travelling by boat from Manila to Boston, she had graduated top of her class and she had been personally sponsored by the president of the Philippines himself. At the age of 24, Del Mundo became the first woman *and* the first Asian person to study at the Harvard Medical School. She already knew what she was going to specialize in: paediatrics. It was the only field, the 1.5-metre- (five-foot) tall doctor once joked, where the patients were smaller than she was. By the time she left America, she had graduated from Harvard Medical School, done her residency at the University of Chicago and gained a master's degree in bacteriology from Boston University.

"I told the Americans who wanted me to stay that I prefer to go home and help the children in my own country," Del Mundo later told a reporter from the Philippine Center for Investigative Journalism (PCIJ). "I know that with my training for five years at Harvard and different medical institutions in America, I can do much."[6]

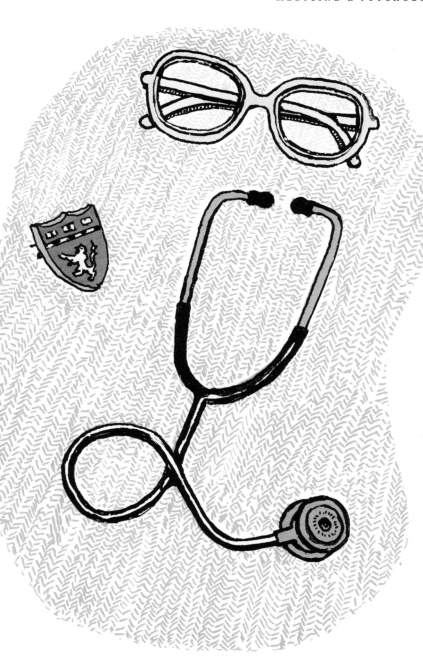

She returned home just in time to see the beginning of the Japanese occupation of the Philippines in 1941. Between 4,000 and 7,000 American men, women and children were interned in an overcrowded POW camp at Santo Tomas University in Manila in dire conditions. Working alongside the International Red Cross, Del Mundo set up a medical centre for sick children, earning her the nickname "The Angel of Santo Tomas".

After Allied forces liberated the Philippines in 1945, Del Mundo set up the first children's hospital in the Philippines. The modest, four-storey building in Quezon City – built partly with her personal savings – was a long time dream of hers. She was a medical intern in her home province of Marinduque when she first realized the dreadful state of children's health in the country. "I saw how many children were not receiving medical attention and how many were dying," she said. "There was no doctor for children and the provincial health officer had no background at all about pediatrics."[7]

Del Mundo knew first-hand of the country's dire need for a specialist children's institution; as a child, she saw four of her seven siblings die. Her little sister Elisa was only seven when she passed away of peritonitis, a treatable abdominal infection. "[Elisa] kept a little notebook where she wrote that she wanted to take up medicine," Del Mundo explained. "When she died, I decided to take her place."[8]

The Children's Memorial Hospital didn't just need her medical expertise to keep it going; it also required funds. Del Mundo poured everything into upgrading its facilities; she even sold her house to pay for a lift and moved into a room on the second floor. But she also knew that it was impossible for the hospital to care for every child in the Philippines. Those living in rural areas or on one of the 7,641 islands scattered through the archipelago often lived too far away from the nearest hospital.

With specially trained teams of medical professionals, Del Mundo roamed far-off parts of the country to treat sick children, check water supplies for disease and offer breastfeeding advice to new mothers. She invented a new incubator for jaundiced and premature babies in areas that lacked access to electricity, made of bamboo and warmed by hot-water bottles to regulate the baby's temperature.

"Medical students must go out into the provinces to see first hand the problems that exist," she said. "Pediatricians must be able to translate medical knowledge into a language their patients will understand. Only in this way can a doctor acquaint their patients with the importance of preventitive as well as curative medicine." It was a mantra she impressed on the generations of medical students she taught in her decades at the University of Santo Tomas and the Far Eastern University in Manila.

For her services to children's health, Del Mundo received the Ramon Magsaysay Award for Public Service in 1977 and continued doing hospital rounds well into her nineties. Over the course of her medical career, she also published 150 scientific papers and authored a medical textbook that remains in use in the Philippines today. Her secret? Her eternal single status. "I'm glad I never got married," she told the PCIJ reporter. "I believe that I've been able to do what I've longed to do because of this."[9]

n receiving her second Nobel Prize in 1911 in Stockholm, the distinguished chemist Marie Curie (1867–1934) told King Gustav V of Sweden that the field of radioactivity she had pioneered was "an infant that I saw being born, which I have contributed to raising with all my strength. The child has grown. It has become beautiful."[10] She could well have been speaking about her daughter, **Irène Joliot-Curie** (1897–1956), the radiochemist who went on to win the Nobel Prize in Chemistry (1935) with her husband and protégé, Frédéric Joliot-Curie.

Irène was born in 1897, the eldest of Marie and Pierre Curie's two daughters. Her grandmother passed away that year and her grandfather, Dr Eugène Curie, came to Paris to look after Irène as Marie continued her doctoral research. From Eugène, Irène developed a keen interest in radical left-wing politics; from her mother, she inherited an enthusiasm for science. Both would go on to shape the course of her life.

Marie clearly had big hopes for the futures of her two children. After Pierre died in a tragic road accident when Irène was a child, Marie and a circle of academic friends created a kind of cooperative home-school, believing that they could offer a more well-rounded education for their offspring than the classroom-bound French school system. Irène's physical education lessons included everything from swimming in the Atlantic Ocean to ice skating and skiing, and Marie herself taught Irène physics, while her mother's university colleagues instructed her in sculpture, Chinese and French literature.

Irène clearly relished the challenge offered by this unusual education. "The derivatives are coming along all right, the inverse functions are adorable," she reported in one letter to her mother. "On the other hand, I can feel my hair stand on end when I think of the theorem of Rolle, and Thomas's formula."[11] She breezed into the Sorbonne at the age of 17, but her college education was derailed by the outbreak of the First World War.

Both mother and daughter were desperate to do their part for France. At the time, X-ray technology was not widely in use in war hospitals; instead, doctors were forced to probe around in wounded soldiers' bodies to find shrapnel and bullets. Marie created radiology stations near the battlefield and a network of cars to service them with equipment.

Midway through studying for her baccalaureate, the teenage Irène joined her mother on the frontlines and quickly gained enough training to head up her own X-ray facility in Belgium. She spent her eighteenth birthday helping doctors find and extract fragments of an artillery shell from a soldier's hand.

After the war, Irène joined her mother at the Radium Institute that Marie had founded in 1914. She wasn't one of the most popular scientists there; her brutal honesty and exacting standards didn't endear her to many, who called her the "Crown Princess", thanks to her mother's position as *la patronne* of the Institute.

Frédéric Joliot, a technical assistant and doctoral student who was assigned to Irène at the Institute, was one of the few able to see past Irène's gruff façade. "I discovered in this girl, whom other people regarded somewhat as a block of ice, an extraordinary person, sensitive and poetic," he wrote. They were married by October 1926 and began working together in what would become one of the most fruitful collaborations in scientific history: together, they would discover artificial radioactivity.

By bombarding aluminium foil with the alpha rays from polonium – the element that Irène's parents had discovered in 1898 – they found that it was possible to create a form of radioactive phosphorus that had never been observed before. This paved the way for the creation of other radioactive isotopes that are still used in the diagnosis and treatment of cancer. Just as her mother had introduced X-ray treatment on the frontlines of the First World War, Irène and her husband's findings blazed a trail in oncology and medicine.

The pair won the Nobel Prize in Chemistry in 1935, but Irène's mother was not there to share in her triumph: Marie had died a few months earlier of aplastic anaemia, thought to have been induced by her exposure to radiation. Though husband and wife had been jointly awarded the Nobel, Frédéric received much more salutary attention in the press than Irène, despite the fact that she had already told a *New York Times* reporter in 1925 that she was of the firm opinion that "men's and women's scientific aptitudes are exactly the same".[12] In an interview with *Journal de la Femme*, she expressed the hope that part of the Nobel win was the "duty to affirm certain ideas that I believe useful for all French women".

In 1936 Irène became the first Undersecretary of State for Scientific Research in a government led by socialist prime minister Léon Blum. Women were still not allowed to vote in France, but the opportunity – which she described as a "sacrifice for the feminist cause"[13] – was too good to miss. Though Irène occupied the position for only three months, she managed to lay the groundwork for an institution that would later become the National Centre for Scientific Research.

When the Nazis seized France in 1940, Frédéric joined the Resistance and became involved with covertly manufacturing radio equipment and bombs, while Irène continued her work at the Radium Institute, which had been renamed the Curie Institute in honour of her mother. Thankfully, Frédéric was never found out, though at one point Irène and her children had to temporarily flee France over the Alps and into Switzerland. But when the Second World War was won against Germany, Frédéric and Irène's communist leanings saw them fall out of favour with wider society. Irène was denied membership of the American Chemical Society and was even briefly detained on Ellis Island when she flew into New York.

But there were other, pressing problems, besides Irène and her husband's social pariah status as "Reds". Like her mother, Irène had been exposed to extraordinary amounts of radiation during her life. Tuberculosis had been discovered during her first pregnancy and in 1956 she was diagnosed with the leukaemia that would eventually take her life. Frédéric passed away of radiation-induced liver disease two years later.

Irène had admired her mother above anyone else and yearned to follow in her footsteps. The Nobel Prize may have been richly deserved, but Irène knew that she had achieved her dream when she and Frédéric made their great discovery. As Frédéric wrote, "I will never forget the expression of intense joy which overtook [Marie] when Irène and I showed her the first 'artificially produced' radioactive element in a little glass tube… This was without a doubt the last great satisfaction of her life."[14]

amilies who send their sons and daughters to medical school aren't rare in the history of medicine, but they are if you belong to an African-American family living in New York City at the turn of the 20th century. **Jane Cooke Wright** (1919–2013) just happened to belong to one such exceptional family.

Her paternal grandfather was born into slavery and qualified as a doctor at the first medical school open to black students in the South; her step-grandfather was the first black man to graduate from Yale Medical College and her father, Dr Louis T Wright, was among the first batch of African-American graduates at Harvard Medical School. When Jane was only one year old, her illustrious surgeon father became the first black man to be appointed as medical staff in a New York hospital, where he set up the Harlem Hospital Cancer Research Foundation in 1948.

Medicine ran in Jane's blood, but it took a while for her to heed its call. Born in Harlem in 1919, she initially fancied herself as an artist and enrolled at Smith College in Massachusetts; after a little gentle persuasion from her father, however, she swapped her paintbrushes for a stethoscope.

Wright soon completed her pre-med course and earned a full academic scholarship to New York Medical College. She impressed her fellow students, supervisors and – most importantly – her father, who asked her to join him at his research centre in 1949.

At the time, oncology – the treatment of cancer – was primarily a surgical speciality. Doctors could remove tumours and growths, but non-surgical methods of treatment were rare. A chemical agent known as nitrogen mustard – the key compound in mustard gas – showed initial promise as a means of attacking the cancerous white blood cells associated with leukaemia, but doctors were still figuring out the dosage and combination of chemicals that worked best.

Both father and daughter relished the challenge; together, they were pioneers in the emerging field of chemotherapy, which Jane described as "the 'Cinderella' of cancer research".[15] She wrote with urgency in a medical paper:

"Cancer is of major concern today because of its high mortality and progressively increasing death toll...It ranks second as a cause of death among men and women of all ages in the United States. Among women between the ages of 30 and 54 years, cancer is the most frequent cause of death."[16]

With Louis in the lab and Jane administering patient trials, they experimented with new anticancer treatments that led to remission in patients with blood cancers such as lymphoma and Hodgkin's disease, and solid tumours such as breast cancer and lung cancer. Their breakthrough drug, methotrexate, is still in use today and is widely regarded as one of the most revolutionary chemotherapy treatments available.

When her father died just four years into their research, Jane took over as director of his centre at the age of 33. In 1955 she was appointed as director of cancer research at the New York University Medical Center, where she made another important discovery. She surgically removed samples of patients' tumours, carefully culturing the cells in petri dishes before experimenting to see which anticancer drug would kill off the most growth. This deceptively simple innovation meant that patients could

be treated with a chemotherapy regime tailored to their specific physiology. Later, she also pioneered a non-surgical way of using a catheter to administer chemo drugs to hard-to-reach organs such as the spleen.

By the time she turned 48, Wright had been appointed by US president Lyndon B Johnson to a presidential commission investigating heart disease, cancer and stroke. She became the highest-ranked black female doctor in the US with a prestigious job as the associate dean of her old alma mater, New York Medical College. She also flew up the ranks of the New York Cancer Society to become its first female president in 1971.

Wright's achievements were exceptional, not least because she worked in a field that was traditionally dominated by men, and white men in particular. Her success is all the more remarkable given that black people still make up only six per cent of all physicians. But Wright was always sanguine about the barriers that life had thrown in her way. "I know I'm a member of two minority groups, but I don't think of myself that way," she told the *New York Post* in 1967. "Sure, a woman has to try twice as hard. But – racial prejudice? I've met very little of it. It could be I met it – and wasn't intelligent enough to recognize it."[17]

Maybe it had something to do with the fact that Wright was born during the Harlem Renaissance, the explosion of art and culture in the New York borough that allowed countless black men and women to dream of a world bigger and better than the one they had been born into. But while the movement can lay claim to artists and poets alike, maybe its biggest success lay in Wright, a self-effacingly modest but groundbreaking scientist.

f you are one of the millions of people worldwide who rely on hay fever medication to get through spring and summer, you have **Ruby Hirose** (1904–1960) to thank. The Japanese-American scientist conducted vital research on treatments for pollen allergies and later helped to develop a vaccine for infantile paralysis, also known as polio. Hirose's accomplishments were no small feat, given that she had to live through the worst years of anti-Japanese sentiment in America: a tide of racism that saw most of her family imprisoned and sent to internment camps.

Hirose's parents were among the thousands of Japanese immigrants who had arrived in the Pacific Northwest at the turn of the 20th century, seeking job prospects and a better future for their children. In the White River Valley near Seattle, her mother and father took on new lives as *issei* (first-generation Japanese immigrants) and leased several hectares of land for a farm.

Growing up as a second-generation immigrant (*nisei*) wasn't easy. Under the law, Japanese and Chinese settlers were not allowed to become US citizens and were barred from owning property. "Mother did not want to go to this place in the beginning but we had no other place to go," she said in an early interview. "Other Japanese have tried to farm the place we are on now and they all failed, so Mother did not see how we could hope to succeed, but it was the only place we could find so we took it."[18]

But Hirose was clearly bound for greater things than tilling the soil. She was the first *nisei* to graduate from her local high school, and earned her bachelor's and master's degrees from the University of Washington. Growing up, Hirose was the only Japanese-American girl in her school and experienced little discrimination against her, but grew dissatisfied with rising anti-Japanese sentiment once she reached her university years. In 1924 she signed up to the Japanese-Christian Student Association (JCSA), a college organization

that was initially set up for foreign-born Japanese students, to "mingle with my own...who understand my problems and frustration".[19]

Hirose joined a JCSA committee that produced a 39-page booklet documenting the issues faced by young *nisei* and their struggle to find acceptance among their parents and wider American society. "If the second generation of Japanese are by nature incapable of being absorbed by the Japanese community and if they are not accepted as Americans by American society," its author Roy Akagi mused, "where should they belong? Thus, they are truly men and women without a country."[20]

Anti-Japanese racism reached its peak when Japan attacked Pearl Harbor and the US declared war against the Axis powers. Thanks to the Second World War, anybody who looked even remotely Japanese was immediately suspect. In 1942 the president, Franklin D Roosevelt, issued an executive order that authorized the incarceration of 117,000 Pacific Northwest and West Coast residents of Japanese descent, two-thirds of them American-born *nisei*. None of the Hirose children had ever set foot in Japan, but Ruby's brother and sister were forced to leave their homes and relocate to internment camps far away. Ruby was spared imprisonment only because she had moved to Ohio.

Despite the hysteria around Japanese immigrants and their families, Hirose's research and academic work flourished. In the Midwest, she completed her doctorate at the University of Cincinnati and was employed by the William S Merrell Laboratories, where she worked to develop serums and antitoxins for the most common and debilitating health conditions. The research Hirose did on polio – once one of the most widespread and feared illnesses among children – helped to pave the way for a vaccine.

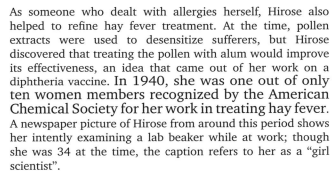

As someone who dealt with allergies herself, Hirose also helped to refine hay fever treatment. At the time, pollen extracts were used to desensitize sufferers, but Hirose discovered that treating the pollen with alum would improve its effectiveness, an idea that came out of her work on a diphtheria vaccine. In 1940, she was one out of only ten women members recognized by the American Chemical Society for her work in treating hay fever. A newspaper picture of Hirose from around this period shows her intently examining a lab beaker while at work; though she was 34 at the time, the caption refers to her as a "girl scientist".

It was only a twist of fate that allowed Hirose a lucky escape from the internment programme that ensnared her family and thousands of others. But she also overcame the struggles of being one of the first generations of American-born Japanese people to become a *nisei* scientific pioneer. In her college years, the JCSA report she contributed to put this almost prophetically: "Men [sic] can only be what he wills and can go only as far as his sense of responsibility will lead him. The members of the second generation should demonstrate to the world that great things will emerge from their ranks through their lives."[21]

hen **Kamala Sohonie** (1912–1998) was born into a family of eminent Indian chemists, it seemed like her future career was all but guaranteed. Unfortunately, she was up against centuries of prejudice that had relegated generations of girls to destinies as housewives and homemakers. As Sohonie put it, an Indian woman was "expected to look after the house, do all the household chores and raise a family. She had no place in the outside world."[22] It was left to Sohonie to break down the door, which she did with a little inspiration from an unexpected source: Mahatma Gandhi.

When Sohonie came top of her undergraduate year at Bombay University, she naturally assumed that she was assured a place at the prestigious Indian Institute of Science (IISc) in Bangalore, where her father and uncle had previously studied chemistry. But her 1933 application was turned down by IISc director C V Raman, a Nobel Prize-winning physicist who reportedly thundered in response: "I am not going to take any girls in my institute!"[23]

Sohonie wasn't going to give up easily. At this point, the Indian independence movement led by Gandhi was almost two decades old. The Gujarat-born political leader espoused a policy of non-violent political resistance called *satyagraha*; just three years earlier, he had led thousands of people on a peaceful 390-kilometre (240-mile) march to protest against an unfair British colonial policy. Sohonie was a fervent admirer of Gandhi and launched her own personal *satyagraha* against the IISc. She began a one-woman sit-in in front of Raman's office, steadfast in the belief that there was no legitimate reason for her rejection.

A reluctant Raman was forced to backtrack and let Sohonie into his institute, but he wasn't going to make it easy for her. Sohonie was admitted on a year-long probation period; she would only be recognized as a full student if Raman was happy with her work. She was also under strict orders not to distract the male students, as if she had come to the IISc only to eye up boys.

"Though Raman was a great scientist, he was very narrow-minded," Sohonie later said. "I can never forget the way he treated me just because I was a woman. Even then, Raman didn't admit me as a regular student. This was a great insult to me. The bias against women was so bad at that time. What can one expect if even a Nobel Laureate behaves in such a way?"[24]

Sohonie threw herself into work and began to carve out her niche in the study of nutritional elements in common foods such as milk, legumes and pulses: a field of biochemistry with wide-ranging implications for public health. After a year, Raman allowed her to stay on as a full student; shortly afterward, he began admitting women into the institute. Sohonie scored a distinction in her course and headed for Cambridge University, England; 14 months later, she submitted a 40-page Ph.D that succinctly outlined how an enzyme called cytochrome C was present in every plant cell and explained its role in plant respiration.

Sohonie's paper astonished her professors and she soon became the first Indian woman to graduate with a doctorate from the university.

By this point, Sohonie had the academic world at her feet and had received several lucrative offers from big pharmaceutical companies, to boot. But she returned to her homeland in 1939, compelled by something deeper than financial success. "She was patriotic and actually returned home from Cambridge to give her might to the freedom movement,"[25] her son Anil Sohonie said, adding that she might even have earned the Nobel if she'd stayed in America.

It was in India that Sohonie's work had the greatest effect. With its millions-strong population, the country had struggled with starvation and famine in the past. As a biochemistry professor at the Royal Institute of Science in Bombay, Sohonie began looking into a popular Indian drink made from the nectar of palm trees: Neera. She discovered that the sweet drink was full of nutrients such as vitamin C and that adding it to the diet of malnourished pregnant women and children could single-handedly turn around their health. It wasn't the only common Indian plant to have startling health benefits; Sohonie found that *gur* (palm) molasses was also a fantastic source of nutrition, and she became a huge advocate for the food as a quick and cheap solution for malnutrition.

For this achievement, she was rewarded with the Rashtrapati Award: one of the highest presidential honours given to civilians. Even today, the Indian government promotes these substances as health foods and subsidizes their production to feed the public. It's no exaggeration to say that Sohonie found a way of helping to feed the nation.

argaret Sanger (1879–1966) was born towards the end of the 19th century in Corning, New York, when condoms weren't just seen as obscene and immoral – they were actually banned. Under the 1873 Comstock Act, it was illegal to send any device or item for the "prevention of conception" through the post.[26] Contraception was a dirty word and Sanger witnessed the effects of that prudishness first-hand. She had ten brothers and sisters and was born into a poor Irish Catholic family to a mother who struggled with her health. By the age of 50, Sanger's mother had died of tuberculosis; her health had crumbled as a result of repeated pregnancy and childbirth. It was little wonder that Sanger once said: "Enforced motherhood is the most complete denial of a woman's right to life and liberty."[27]

Sanger was determined to leave her birthplace and found her escape by qualifying as a nurse in 1902 and marrying an architect named William Sanger that same year. By 1910, Sanger and her family had moved to the bright lights of New York City and discovered their place among the radical intellectuals and bohemians of Greenwich Village. Change bristled in the air. A new political culture was flourishing around them: one that was concerned with social inequality and had a vision of a better world. Sanger – now a mother of three – signed up to the Liberal Club and joined the Socialist Party of New York, travelling to New Jersey and Massachusetts to take part in labour strikes.

It was around this time that she also began working as a midwife and nurse in some of the most deprived neighbourhoods in the city. On the Lower East Side, she saw women forced into destitution and despair by the same forces that had driven her mother to the grave.

They had no choice over their reproductive health; like a lightning strike, pregnancy was something that simply happened to them, whether they wanted it to or not.

One day, a doctor that Sanger worked with advised a patient that she should force her husband to sleep on the roof if she didn't want another child: "You can't have your cake and eat it too!" he laughed.[28] In Sanger's autobiography, she wrote that the desperate woman pleaded with her after the doctor left the room: "Tell me the secret – and I'll never breathe it to a soul!"[29] Sanger had no answer to give. Several weeks later, the woman was dead: she had contracted a fatal infection after attempting to self-induce an abortion.

The death of this patient weighed heavily on Sanger's soul; she stayed up all night, unable to stop thinking of the injustice of it all. It would set her on a path to become one of the world's leading medical pioneers in contraception and sexual health.

In 1912 Sanger started writing a column for the *New York Call*, a left-wing daily newspaper, in which she dispensed advice about sexual health and contraception. Two years later, she began publishing *The Woman Rebel*, a feminist journal that primarily advocated better contraception and a woman's right to choose. "I believed it was my duty to place motherhood on a higher level than enslavement and accident," she said.[30]

Just a few months later, the Comstock Act came crashing down on her head. Sanger was indicted on nine counts of sending birth-control-related material through the post. But she didn't wait around to be sent to prison: the day before her trial, she fled the country and made for Europe. In the Netherlands, she visited a family planning clinic and was convinced by the effectiveness of the diaphragm. When the charges against her were dropped in 1916, she returned to set up the first birth control clinic in Brooklyn, New York. Her dream of a network of centres that offered a range of contraceptive services was later realized when she set up the American Birth Control League in 1921 – now known as Planned Parenthood – and made its mission global with the 1952 formation of the International Planned Parenthood Foundation. She was also involved behind the scenes in scientific research, supporting and raising funds for newer and more advanced contraceptive methods: efforts that eventually led to the creation of the Pill.

Over her lifetime, Sanger was arrested, hounded out of her own country and even threatened with jail for what she believed in. But she lived to see her life's work vindicated: in 1965, a year before she died, the US Supreme Court ruled that a state contraception ban violated the right to privacy, thereby legalizing birth control. She never lost faith that the country would come around to her belief that contraceptive choice would mean freeing women from the cycle of childbirth and poverty.

"I was convinced we must care about people; we must reach out to help them in their despair...For these beliefs I was denounced, arrested, I was in and out of police courts and higher courts, and indictments hung over my life for several years. But nothing could alter my beliefs. Because I saw these as truths, I stubbornly stuck to my convictions."[31]

f you've ever been unlucky enough to have chickenpox, shingles or herpes, your doctor might have prescribed you aciclovir: an antiviral medication that the World Health Organization considers one of the safest and most important essential medicines in any healthcare system. And you have **Gertrude B Elion** (1918–1999) – Trudy to her friends and family – to thank for it.

Elion was born in New York City, the first child of a Lithuanian dentist and a Polish immigrant. Her Bronx upbringing as a "child with an insatiable thirst for knowledge",[32] as she put it, meant that she excelled at school and could have easily picked any subject when it came to choosing her degree. That summer, however, her beloved grandfather passed away of stomach cancer. "The suffering I witnessed during his last months made a great impression on me," she said. "I decided that a worthwhile goal for my life would be to do something to help cure this terrible disease."[33]

She didn't quite discover a cure for cancer, but she came close. The drugs that Elion developed over the course of her decades-long career in pharmaceutical research and medicine included treatments for leukaemia, gout, rheumatoid arthritis, malaria and HIV/AIDS, as well as immunosuppressant drugs that stop the body from rejecting donated organs. She was given the Nobel Prize in Physiology or Medicine in 1988 – and she did this all without a doctorate.

In 1944, biochemist Dr George H Hitchings – with whom she would later share the Nobel Prize – employed her as his assistant at the Burroughs Wellcome research lab. It was a once-in-a-lifetime opportunity in more ways than one. When Elion had graduated from Hunter College in 1937 with her chemistry degree, nobody wanted to employ women in the lab: "They wondered why in the world I wanted to be a chemist when no women were doing that," she recalled. "The world was not waiting for me."[34] Instead, she took on a series of teaching jobs at a school and a hospital while working on her master's degree in the evenings. But the advent of the Second World War changed everything: all men between the ages of 21 and 35 were conscripted for military service, leaving the factories, businesses and research labs of America empty of staff. Women like Elion answered the call.

"My thirst for knowledge stood me in good stead in that laboratory, because Dr Hitchings permitted me to learn as rapidly as I could and to take on more and more responsibility when I was ready for it...From being solely an organic chemist, I soon became very much involved in microbiology and in the biological activities of the compounds I was synthesizing."[35]

In the 1940s, Elion's fiance passed away of a bacterial infection that would have been easily treated by penicillin (the drug was only developed after his death). The tragedy served only to underscore her desire to develop drugs that would treat the sick.

Elion was still desperate to get her Ph.D and spent long evenings commuting between home, the lab and night classes at Brooklyn Polytechnic Institute. Eventually her professors gave her an ultimatum: commit full-time to the doctorate, or give it up. She chose to stay at Burroughs Wellcome, where she remained for the next 39 years and rose to become head of department of experimental therapy in 1967. "Years later," she said, "when I received three honorary doctorate degrees from George Washington University, Brown University and the University of Michigan, I decided that perhaps that decision had been the right one after all."[36]

At Burroughs Wellcome, she blazed a new trail in the development of drugs. When it came to tackling viruses such as herpes simplex and herpes zoster, the majority of scientists believed that most antivirals would indiscriminately attack the DNA of healthy cells, too. After years of research, she came up with acyclovir, which stops the virus from multiplying with no effect on the body's own cells. It was the development of medicines like this that led to the Nobel Prize for her and Hitchings. "In awarding them the Nobel," one of their colleagues at the lab said, "the prize committee said that their work was so important that each of the drugs for which they were honored could have won the prize in itself...This record of drug discovery is unlikely ever to be equaled."[37]

During her career, Elion received 23 honorary degrees and never stopped trying to inspire medical students and young women to take her path. In her notes, she jotted down the motivational speech she often delivered to any aspiring scientists: "There may be those who try to deter you and discourage you along the way. But keep your eye on the goal. And in the words of Admiral Farragut, 'Damn the torpedoes, full speed ahead!'"[38]

hen Dr **Helen Rodríguez-Trías** (1929–2001) was a medical intern in San Juan, Puerto Rico, she witnessed the inequalities in women's health for herself. It was the 1950s and abortion was still two decades away from being legalized in the US. Thanks to Puerto Rico's relatively liberal law on terminations, those with money would head to abortion clinics in the US territory:

"I saw that anybody who could afford an abortion could get a perfectly fine one. It would be written up as an appendectomy… If a poor woman needed an abortion, she came to the University Hospital in the middle of the night and said she had fallen and was having a miscarriage."[39]

If a woman was extremely desperate, she could resort to self-inducing a miscarriage: a risky procedure that could lead to a fatal infection. On the ward at San Juan's University Hospital, where Rodríguez-Trías was training as a doctor, a mother of five passed away after attempting to perform her own abortion.

For Rodríguez-Trías, who wanted to go into medicine as it "combined the things I loved the most, science and people", this was unacceptable.[40] As a medical resident, she founded Puerto Rico's first health centre for the care of newborns, which led to a 50 per cent decrease in the infant mortality rate of children at University Hospital.

Rodríguez-Trías was born in New York City in 1929 and her family instilled in her a strong sense of Puerto Rican identity. After qualifying as a doctor in San Juan, she returned to New York and began working as the head of paediatrics at Lincoln Hospital, which predominantly served the poor working-class Puerto Rican community in the Bronx.

Unlike many of her non-Puerto Rican colleagues at the hospital, she understood how poverty and lack of opportunity in the Latino community contributed directly to poor health: "I try to emphasize the need to improve health conditions: Where we work, where we live, what our environment is like," she said. "All of these elements in life are determinants and definers of our health."[41]

In the 1970s, Rodríguez-Trías joined the American women's health movement and became a leading figure in the national campaign to end sterilization abuse. In the US and its territories abroad, poor and disadvantaged women of colour were often coerced or tricked by the government into agreeing to permanent sterilization. In Puerto Rico alone, a grotesque US policy on population control saw a third of women of childbearing age sterilized over a period of 30 years. Many of the women involved were told by doctors that sterilization was the only birth control option available. Back on US shores, the federal government frequently threatened to remove women's benefits if they failed to comply with the procedure. In the South, the involuntary sterilization of African-American women was so widespread that it was nicknamed the "Mississippi appendectomy"; in one horrifying case from Alabama, two black girls, aged 12 and 14, with learning disabilities went into a clinic for routine contraception and came out robbed of their ability to have children. Doctors told their mother that they were being given a contraceptive shot.

As Rodríguez-Trías began speaking out about sterilization abuse, more women and survivors started to object in voices of outrage and desperation. She remembered going on radio shows to raise awareness of the issue: "Someone would call in and say, 'Three years ago, I was told I had something wrong with my uterus and they took it out and I don't have any children and I'm only 22 years old and I don't know what's happening.'"[42] Her advice to women was, "Be informed, read all you can, talk to others, know your rights, and speak up."[43]

Rodríguez-Trías co-founded the Committee to End Sterilization Abuse and the Committee for Abortion Rights and Against Sterilization Abuse, and lobbied for stricter federal guidelines on the procedure. To stop the abuse of the past, she helped to create rules that specifically protected the rights of women patients, including a 30-day wait between the signing of consent and the actual operation, and a guarantee that counselling and forms would be provided in their language of choice.

"I think you have to have the heart to say, 'I care a lot about this issue'...That's the first thing: feeling committed. The second thing is to look around to see who else feels like you do and thinks like you do, or if there's something going on already that you can become part of."[44]

After she won the battle on sterilization rights, Rodríguez-Trías headed up the New York State AIDS Institute and the New York Women in AIDS Task Force in the 1980s, focused on making sure that even the most marginalized and poorest communities could access help at the height of the epidemic. She also became the first Latina woman to lead the American Public Health Association, the world's oldest group of public health professionals. In recognition of her decades of work in making healthcare available to all – regardless of race, gender or class – then-president Bill Clinton awarded her the Presidential Citizen's Medal in 2001.

nervous Dr **Elisabeth Kübler-Ross** (1926–2004) first began teaching medical students at the University of Colorado in Denver when she filled in for a professor whose lectures were enormously popular. Her teaching style was unconventional, to say the least. Instead of holding forth at the lectern or handing out assignments, Kübler-Ross invited a 16-year-old girl with terminal leukaemia to meet her class. "Ask her some questions," she told her students.

The would-be doctors tentatively quizzed the teen about her medical regime until she lost her temper. *Why wasn't anybody talking to her about how she was going to die?* she asked. The dying girl's outburst left the students in tears. "Why won't people tell you the truth?" she said accusingly.[45] She would die before ever getting the chance to grow up; why weren't any of her doctors talking to her about that? The dying girl's words moved the class to tears. "Now you're acting like human beings, instead of scientists," Kübler-Ross said approvingly.[46] The Swiss-born psychiatrist's deeply empathetic, person-centred approach to medicine would go on to revolutionize how we look at death.

Kübler-Ross was born in Switzerland as the first of triplets. She had an early encounter with death when a family friend, severely injured from a fall, invited his neighbours and associates to visit him on his deathbed. He asked them to take care of his wife and children after he died, showing no trace of fear in the face of death. "My last visit with him filled me with great pride and joy," she said later.[47]

Kübler-Ross was 12 when she told her parents that she wanted to be a doctor. After she left school, she volunteered in Europe as a relief worker and helped to treat Second World War refugees. At a Polish concentration camp, she found hundreds of butterflies etched into its walls: a symbol of hope amid inconceivable violence. This experience solidified her desire to become a psychiatrist and help people better understand death.

In 1958 Kübler-Ross moved to the US and began training as a psychiatrist in New York, where she was shocked by how doctors routinely treated dying patients. According to Kübler-Ross, medical staff "shunned and abused" those with terminal illnesses.[48] At the time, palliative care was in its infancy; many doctors refused to face up to the truth that their patients might be dying. Keenly aware that people approaching death needed specialized care, she began to create counselling programmes that would accord dying individuals the respect and health care that they deserved. She asked:

"What is it like to be dying?" Not from the nurse's point of view, nor from the doctor's, nor the family's, but from the patient's point of view: what is it like? Because, if we have some idea of what the answer might be, then we're going to be in a better position to help."[49]

When she was appointed as an assistant professor at the University of Chicago Medical School, she led a controversial series of seminars where terminally ill patients were interviewed about their thoughts and feelings about death. She hoped that the doctors watching would learn something about how to better treat their other patients. From these sessions, she developed the theory that would go down in history: the five stages of grief. In her book *On Death and Dying* (1969), Kübler-Ross proposed that people would travel through five phases before coming to terms with their forthcoming death: denial, anger, bargaining, depression and finally acceptance.

"Dying patients generally go through a series of stages," she wrote. "The stages don't always follow one another; they overlap sometimes and sometimes they go back and forth."[50] In a world where all talk of dying was frowned upon, the book became a bestseller, cementing Kübler-Ross's reputation as the leading expert on thanatology, the study of death. In her later work, she detailed how the five stages could also apply to bereavement and emotional trauma, such as after a devastating divorce.

Medical experts now question the accuracy of Kübler-Ross's theory, pointing out that her sessions and subsequent conclusions lacked scientific rigour. Later on in life, she also grew convinced of the existence of life beyond death after meeting a patient who had been through a near-death experience. Kubler-Ross dabbled with spirit guides and even began doing business with a man who claimed to be a spiritual healer. (He was later outed as a fraud and investigated over allegations of sexual misconduct.) These professional associations and her new-found eccentricity damaged her credibility, and she struggled to regain the respect of the medical profession.

Despite her late swerve into spiritualism, Kübler-Ross remained a tireless advocate for the rights of terminally ill patients and inspired the work of countless hospices. Her work gave a voice to the dying and dragged the taboo subject of death into the sunlight, forcing the medical establishment to improve the way it treated dying people and their families. Kübler-Ross never gave up on finding death's deepest and truest meaning. "For those who seek to understand it, death is a highly creative force," she said. "The highest spiritual values of life can originate from the thought and study of death."[51]

eta Hollingworth (1886–1939) spent her childhood on the wild and open plains of Nebraska, and often spoke of the benefits of growing up on a seemingly limitless frontier. "To grow up on their expanse means to 'see in long stretches,' to scorn boundaries, to go 'free' all one's life," she said. It was only when she left the prairie that she encountered the crushing and unjust gender norms of the modern century, and she would spend most of her life using science to prove these stereotypes wrong.

Born in 1886, Hollingworth was a precocious child who could sit up at 21 weeks of age and say "Mama" and "Papa" by the time she reached her seventh month. Her early childhood, as she put it, consisted of "Texas longhorns, Sioux Indians, blizzards, sod-houses and the one-room schoolhouse" where she received an excellent education.[52] After graduating from the University of Nebraska at the age of 19, she worked as a schoolteacher for two years before relocating to New York to marry an ex-classmate, Henry Hollingworth, who was working as a graduate assistant to a Columbia University professor. So far, so easy, but Leta received a rude shock when she realized that no public school in New York would hire a married woman as a teacher. Left cooped up at home and confined to the drudgery of housework, she soon felt the sting of resentment. Henry wrote sympathetically of her frustrations as a newlywed:

"Almost always she effectually stifled her own eager longing for intellectual activity like that of her husband…Day after day, and many long evenings, she led her solitary life in the meagerly furnished quarters, while he was away at regular duties… 'Staying at home eating a lone pork chop' was the way she sometimes facetiously described her experience in these days."[53]

At that time, however, women weren't just expected to stay at home; it was genuinely thought that it was all that they were capable of doing. Some of science's leading thinkers even claimed to have found empirical proof that the female intellect did not match up to that of the male. French social psychologist Gustave Le Bon declared in 1879 that "all psychologists who have studied the intelligence of women…recognize today that they represent the most inferior forms of human evolution and that they are closer to children and savages than to an adult, civilized man."[54]

If there was one thing Hollingworth loved, it was a challenge. After she and her husband had saved up enough money to send her to graduate school at Columbia, she decided to take on these supposed truths about female intelligence one by one, finding that the so-called variability hypothesis lay at their root. Men, the argument went, exhibited wider variability in all aspects than women and were equally capable of great intellect and immense stupidity. Women, however, were limited in their range of ability and this was why there were fewer of them hailed as geniuses or locked up in mental institutions and prisons.

Hollingworth challenged this orthodoxy step by step. In 1913 she worked as a clinical psychologist carrying out intelligence tests on individuals at the Clearing-House for Mental Defectives. Over the course of assessing some 1,000 people with learning difficulties, she found out that there were more young men than young women in the institution, but that the reverse was true among the older demographic. This had nothing to do with the intelligence of either sex, but occurred because such boys were identified as a burden on the family and sent away, while girls were retained in the home to serve as domestic help until they reached old age. In short, their social contexts had more to do with them ending up in the Clearing-House than their actual intellectual ability. This was a theme that Hollingworth would emphasize consistently in all her research:

"The lives of men and women are lived under conditions so different as to constitute practically different environments…We should expect to find adult males more variable than adult females, because the males are free to follow a great variety of trades, professions and industries, while women have been confined to the single

occupation of housekeeping...A woman of natural herculean strength does not wash dishes, cook meals, or rear children much more successfully than a woman of ordinary muscle. But a man of natural herculean strength is free to abandon carpentry or agriculture and become a prize fighter or a blacksmith."[55]

Another common belief about the ability of women was that their periods made them feeble in body and mind, and Hollingworth staked her doctoral dissertation on the premise that they didn't. Over three months, she administered tests on motor ability and mental faculty to a group of men and women, discovering that there was zero difference in performance at any point in any of their menstrual cycles. It was groundbreaking research such as this that led to Hollingworth's reputation as the "scientific pillar" of the women's rights movement: a reputation that, given her membership of the Women's Suffrage Party, she must have been delighted to receive.[56]

After gaining her doctorate, Hollingworth focused on the psychology of gifted children and how best to utilize and develop their talents, even founding her own school to put her theories into practice. Much of what we now take for granted regarding how to nurture intelligence in children is due to Hollingworth's work. At her Speyer School in Manhattan, creativity and independent study were paramount, and teachers guided children to design their own curriculum and investigate their chosen topics with as much freedom as they desired. For Hollingworth, it wasn't simply enough to be born smart: society had to nourish the minds of women and children, just as she had sought to enrich her own and, in the process, challenge the orthodoxy of those around her: "I was intellectually curious, I worked hard, was honest except for those benign chicaneries which are occasionally necessary when authority is stupid, disliked waste, and was never afraid to undertake an experiment or to change my mind. My family motto, translated from the Latin, reads "I love to test"."[57]

Elements &
genetics

n surveying the history of scientific accomplishment, it's easy to feel irritated by the long list of people who showed promise early on in their lives: the wunderkinds who were already reading Sir Isaac Newton's work in the original Latin by age eight, or the geniuses who were creating experimental set-ups before they turned twelve. But if there's anything that **Nettie Stevens's** (1861–1912) story shows, it's that age has no bearing on achievement.

Stevens was born into a middle-class New England family in 1861, and counted herself fortunate to be able to attend school and graduate at 19 with a career in teaching ahead of her. But the life of a schoolteacher was never going to satisfy Stevens, though her obvious passion for her subject shone through in the classroom. "How could you think your questions would bother me?" she once told a nervous student. "They never will, so long as I keep my enthusiasm for biology; and that, I hope will be as long as I live."[1]

After spending most of the next two decades teaching, scrimping on her hard-earned wages to pursue further education and then returning to work to save some more, Stevens finally made it to Stanford University in 1896 as she turned 35. By the time she completed her doctorate in 1903 at Pennsylvania's Bryn Mawr College, 41-year-old Stevens's new career as a scientist was in full swing: she had published nine papers, been awarded a biology scholarship and was sponsored to travel abroad to study in Italy and Germany. One of her essays won a $1,000 top prize from an organization dedicated to promoting women in science.

Despite being a relatively small women's college, Bryn Mawr was home to a brilliant biology department undertaking cutting-edge research into chromosomes, the thread-like coil of DNA that carries our genetic information. Today we know that the X and Y chromosomes are what determine our sex. But back then people attributed this to everything from the temperature and the season (boys were thought more likely to be born during winter) to the mother's diet: better eating habits, it was proposed, resulted in females.[2] In 1900, however, Gregor Mendel's laws of inheritance had been rediscovered and the scientific world was abuzz with the idea that genetic traits – like the colour of seeds in Mendel's pea plant experiments – could be passed on through successive generations. Could sex, too, be an inherited trait? Stevens was determined to find out.

Her plans were almost scuppered when she ran out of money. Writing to the Carnegie Institution of Washington, she requested financial support so that she could experience the "freedom from [the] anxiety over the money question".[3] Her advisor and the head of the biology faculty at Bryn Mawr, Thomas H Morgan, urged the Institution to sponsor one of his most talented students. "Miss Stevens has not only the training but she has also the natural talent that is I believe much harder to find," he wrote. "She has an independent and original mind and does thoroughly whatever she undertakes. I fear to say more lest it may appear that I am overstating her case."[4]

Carnegie awarded Stevens the grant in 1904 and she plunged blissfully into full-time research. When she began investigating the tricky question of sex determination, she

set her sights small: on *Tenebrio molitor*, otherwise known as the common mealworm. When examining the female and male insect under a microscope, she realized that the female always had 20 large chromosomes, while the male always possessed 19 large chromosomes and a single small one: what we now know as X and Y chromosomes respectively. It stood to reason, Stevens argued, that the presence of the small chromosome in sperm was what determined male offspring. "This seems to be a clear case of sex determination," she wrote in *Studies in Spermatogenesis*.[5]

In a cruel twist of fate, Stevens was actually one of two scientists who had discovered the mystery of sex determination. In the same year, Edmund Beecher Wilson at Columbia University had arrived at similar conclusions, thanks to his work on *Hemiptera* bugs. Even though Stevens presented a more convincing argument and was more far sighted in grasping the extensive implications of her hypothesis, it is Wilson's name that is now more commonly associated with the discovery.

Stevens did not live to see her hypothesis confirmed or to witness how it revolutionized our understanding of biology and sex. Two years after she was ranked among the top 1,000 scientists in *American Men of Science*, a kind of Who's Who of the industry, she passed away. Bryn Mawr still holds on to her Carl Zeiss microscope, which is affectionately nicknamed "Nettie Maria" in her honour.

da Noddack (1869–1978) was never supposed to be a scientist. Her father had groomed her for a job in his small varnish factory on the Rhine and Ida had dutifully studied organic chemistry in preparation for the family business. Luckily, destiny had other plans for her and it would eventually lead to her discovering a new element, named after the river close to where she grew up.

In 1922, she met Walter Noddack and found in him a kindred spirit. The German chemist was three years older than Ida and was the director of the chemistry lab at the Physico-Technical Research Agency in Berlin at the time. Two years later, she left her job in the lab of an AEG turbine factory and joined Walter, adopting his quest to discover two unknown elements that remained in the periodic table: a chase that had eluded many scientists before them.

For most of the 19th century, scientists stumbled upon new elements more or less by accident. But in 1896, Russian chemist Dmitri Mendeleev published what later became the modern periodic table. By arranging the known elements of the time in increasing order of atomic mass, he found that he was able to group them into six columns. But there were also spaces in his table, which he theorized were the result of missing elements.

By Ida Noddack's time, there were only two left unclaimed: Elements 43 and 75, both in the manganese group. The race was on. "From spring 1923 on," Noddack remembered, "I spent ten months from early morning to late night in the Berlin State Library ploughing through almost 100 years of literature in inorganic chemistry."[6]

Scientists had previously scoured manganese ore for the elements, but their rigorous studies of the field led Ida and Walter to believe that the missing two would bear little resemblance to manganese. Instead, they looked at elements that were horizontal neighbours to the two mystery elements: metals like molybdenum and tungsten. Ida called on her factory connections to access cutting-edge X-ray spectroscopy equipment and analysed more than 400 enriched samples in search of Element 43 and 75.

Finally, in June 1925, they hit the jackpot with a sample of a Norwegian columbite ore and the help of X-ray specialist Otto Berg. It was Element 75, one of the two missing elements. They named it rhenium after the Rhine, the European river that flows through the Swiss Alps, Germany and the Netherlands. It took them a year – and 660 kilos (104 stones) of ore – to extract a single gram (three-hundredths of an ounce) of the new element. Ida Noddack outlined the major discovery in an address to the Society of German Chemists – the first woman to do so – and became the third woman ever nominated for the Nobel Prize.

By rights, the discovery should have made Ida and Walter international sensations. However, they made the fatal error of trying to kill two birds with one stone. They also claimed that they had discovered Element 43, which they named masurium. But Ida and Walter failed to extract any masurium, and when other scientists tried to replicate their initial results, their attempts fell flat. Their chosen name for the element also proved controversial. It was ostensibly named after Masuria, Walter's birthplace in East Prussia (now northern Poland), but other scientists believed that the name masurium had overwhelmingly nationalistic overtones, harking back to a battle during the First World War in which Germany defeated Russia. (After the Second World War, Walter was exonerated of any involvement with National Socialism by a denazification court.) Either way, the disputed element tarnished Ida and Walter's reputation, and Element 43 was properly discovered in 1936 by researchers at the University of Palermo.

Ida married Walter in 1926 and ran straight into sexist employment legislation, designed to keep married women out of jobs. After the First World War, Germany had passed a law that forced women to resign from their jobs after they wed, lest they deprive a hard-up man of the position. As a result, Ida would spend the following decades dependent on her husband's connections and position to ensure access to equipment, labouring for most of her career as an unpaid researcher, a glorified assistant to her husband. But in fact, Ida and Walter's partnership was utterly collaborative, and Ida coined the term *Arbeitsgemeinschaft*, which translates as "work unit", to describe it.

But even though both partners saw each other as absolute scientific equals, the rest of the world didn't see it that way. In the 1930s, Noddack became interested in a newly emerging field: nuclear physics. Italian physicist Enrico Fermi claimed to have discovered Element 93, a new transuranium element, by bombarding uranium with neutrons. The periodic table was, of course, Noddack's speciality and she could see immediately where Fermi had gone wrong. "It is conceivable, that the bombardment of heavy nuclei by neutrons cause them to break up into larger fragments, which would be isotopes of known elements, but now close neighbours of the irradiated element," she concluded.[7] In other words, Fermi wasn't producing a new element; he was observing nuclear fission. She put the idea forth in a paper titled "On Element 93".

Noddack had no formal position or recognition at a scientific institution, and she was completely derided by leading scientists such as Otto Hahn, who were convinced of the existence of transuranium elements. Noddack said later:

"When in 1935 or 1936 my husband suggested to Hahn by word of mouth that he should make some reference, in his lectures and publications, to my criticism of Fermi's experiments, Hahn answered that he did not want to make me look ridiculous as my assumption of the bursting of the uranium nucleus into larger fragments was really absurd."[8]

In the end, it was two women who elucidated the theory of nuclear fission: Ida Noddack, who first glimpsed it in 1934, and Lise Meitner, who worked it out four years later (see page 132). When the discovery of nuclear fission was finally claimed by Hahn and Fritz Strassman (see page 135), Noddack wrote to a scientific journal to state that she had suggested that the nucleus of uranium had been split some years earlier. Both men refused to comment, leading the journal's editor to note regretfully: "Otto Hahn and Fritz Strassman informed us that they have neither the time nor the interest to answer the preceding note... They have their own opinion on the correctness of the views of Frau Ida Noddack and the way she expressed them to the peers."[9]

n 1962 James Watson and Francis Crick jointly received the Nobel Prize in Physiology or Medicine for the discovery of DNA with the help of one woman: **Rosalind Franklin** (1920–1958), who had died four years earlier of cancer. It would be decades until the true extent of her role was discovered, thanks to Watson's negative comments about her in his autobiography, *The Double Helix* (1968).

The great scientist, who Watson dismissed as a "belligerent" bluestocking unable to "keep her emotions under control",[10] was born in London in 1920. "All her life," her mother later said, "Rosalind knew exactly where she was going, and at sixteen, she took science for her subject."[11] She studied at Newnham College, Cambridge, at the same time as Joan Clarke, who would go on to become a brilliant codebreaker at Bletchley Park (see page 160). Like Clarke, Franklin played her part in the war effort. By the time she turned 26, she had published five scientific papers from her work at the British Coal Utilisation Research Association (BCURA), where she undertook vital research that helped to improve the gas masks used by soldiers.

But it was at King's College in London where Franklin made one of her most significant contributions to science: the discovery of the unique double-helix shape of DNA. Two research teams were locked in a race to unveil the building blocks that make up all life on earth: one at Cambridge, consisting of Watson and Crick, and another at King's College. Thanks to her time previously working as a researcher under X-ray crystallographer Jacques Mering, at the Laboratoire Centrale des Services Chimiques de l'Etat in Paris, Franklin was an expert in X-ray crystallography, a scientific technique that uses X-rays to determine the structure of a crystal. One of her former colleagues described the photographs she produced from her work as "among the most beautiful of any substances ever taken".[12]

But while Franklin thrived in the egalitarian and collegiate atmosphere of French academia, the same was not true in staid, stuffy England. At King's, this was best exemplified by the fact that men and women had separate common rooms. (The women's, of course, was the shabbier of the two.) That didn't sit well with Franklin. Neither did the fact that the director of King's Medical Research Council (MRC), John Randall, had told her that she would be the sole researcher looking into DNA, without mentioning that Maurice Wilkins, a molecular biologist and physicist, would also be working on the problem.

The two were thrown together by an unfortunate omission on Randall's part and immediately wanted little to do with each other. Wilkins was reserved and timid, while Franklin was formidably direct. The general consensus at King's was that Franklin had become "too French".[13] But she was not interested in being popular in the lab; she was determined to get down to work. Assisted by a graduate student named Raymond Gosling, Franklin meticulously extracted individual DNA fibres from a sample for X-ray analysis. By toying with different levels of humidity in the lab, she realized that there wasn't just a single form of DNA: there were two. At 95 per cent humidity, the DNA sample stretched like a piece of warm toffee, resulting in a longer molecule that she and Gosling called the "B" form. "Either the structure is a big helix or a smaller helix consisting of several chains,"[14] she mused.

Was Franklin well on her way to cracking the double-helix structure of DNA? Perhaps. But she was an exacting and precise scientist; first she wanted to confirm that the helix proposal held true of DNA's drier and more crystalline form.

Unfortunately, her professional relationship with Wilkins derailed her plan. When Watson visited King's, Wilkins let slip Franklin's "B" form discovery in the middle of a diatribe about his recalcitrant colleague, and even pulled out a high-quality photograph of the pattern to prove his point.

"The instant I saw the picture my mouth fell open and my pulse began to race," Watson recounted in his memoirs.[15] Photograph 51, as the print was known, set Watson and Crick well ahead of Franklin on the path of discovery. Franklin also helped to nudge them along to another crucial breakthrough without even knowing it. Thanks to another MRC-funded scientist, an unpublished paper that Franklin had prepared for a government committee in summary of her DNA work ended up in the hands of the two Cambridge scientists. Watson was remarkably frank about it: "Rosy, of course, did not directly give us her data. For that matter, no one at King's realized they were in our hands."[16]

On 25 April 1953, Watson and Crick announced the double-helix discovery, just as Franklin was in the middle of a transfer to Birkbeck College, where she swapped the study of DNA for viruses such as polio. She never disputed Watson and Crick's DNA model and in fact enjoyed a good friendship with Crick and his wife, Odile. It wasn't until Watson's book that the full extent of Franklin's contribution to the discovery of DNA became clear and, for all his grumpiness about her, even Watson paid her a grudging respect for the uncompromising approach that had helped him and Crick on the way to a world-changing discovery. As he put it: "[It] reflected first-rate science, not the outpourings of a misguided feminist."[17]

hen **Rita Levi-Montalcini** (1909–2012) turned a hundred in 2009, she was still going to work every day at the European Brain Research Institute (EBRI) in Rome, which she had founded seven years prior. As a colleague commented to a journalist, Levi-Montalcini's boundless energy could only be due to one thing: her daily dose of nerve growth factor (NGF), which she administered in the form of eye drops.[18] Why wouldn't she? After all, she was the one who discovered it.

Born in 1909 into a Jewish family governed by Victorian morals, Levi-Montalcini overcame an incredible number of obstacles in pursuit of her scientific career. "It was a very patriarchal society, and I simply resented, from early childhood, that women were reared in such a way that everything was decided by the man," she told *Scientific American*.[19] But when her father decided that Rita and her two sisters would skip university to focus on homemaking, something in her rebelled.

"At 20, I realized that I could not possibly adjust to a feminine role as conceived by my father, and asked him permission to engage in a professional career," she said. Levi-Montalcini's father listened intently to her request and finally acceded. "In eight months I filled my gaps in Latin, Greek and mathematics, graduated from high school, and entered medical school in Turin."[20]

Her triumph in graduating with distinction from the University of Turin was short-lived. Two years after she decided to go into medical research, the fascist dictator Benito Mussolini passed anti-Semitic laws that expelled Jewish people from all academic and cultural institutions. Lesser scientists would have been scared off by Mussolini's threats of prison or execution, but Levi-Montalcini was undeterred. She set up a lab in her bedroom at her parents' house and began to research her chosen field of nerve development.

Levi-Montalcini had read a paper by Viktor Hamburger, a leading neurobiologist based in St Louis, Missouri, who was using chick embryos to work out how newly developing nerve tissue knew how to reach its final destination from its starting point in the spinal cord. She wanted to replicate Hamburger's experiments, and while she didn't have access to a lab or a university, Levi-Montalcini did possess boundless ingenuity.

She approached farmers and told them that she was looking for eggs for her children; she fashioned her own surgical equipment out of miniature tools, such as a watchmaker's tiny tweezers. She used these to surgically excise the budding limbs of the embryo to work out why nerve cells didn't proliferate in these areas of amputation as much as they did in others.

Levi-Montalcini proposed that it was because these nerves were actually dying off: some nutrient that would have ordinarily been produced by the limb wasn't able to do its job to encourage the differentiation of nerve cells. It wasn't long before her research brought her to the attention of the international scientific community, including Hamburger himself. After the Second World War came to an end, he invited her to join him for a few months at Washington University in St Louis to continue her embryo research. She ended up staying there for three decades.

When one of Hamburger's graduate students stitched a chick embryo to a mouse sarcoma tumour and found that embryonic nerves started growing uncontrollably, Levi-Montalcini began to suspect that the tumour and all those limb buds she had excised in Turin were both secreting the same factor. With the biochemist Stanley Cohen, she worked for years to identify and isolate the mysterious nerve-boosting nutrient, which they named nerve growth factor (NGF). She even smuggled two tumour-ridden mice in her handbag on a plane to Rio de Janeiro, where an old student ran one of the only labs in the world with the equipment to confirm her hypothesis.

Levi-Montalcini and Cohen were finally proven right in 1959, when they developed an antiserum that worked against NGF and effectively eradicated nerve growth when administered to newborn mice. They shared the Nobel Prize in 1986, and their discovery has been instrumental for the research and treatment of diseases such as Alzheimer's and cancer.

For Levi-Montalcini, the Nobel in Physiology or Medicine was a means to an end. She used it to speak up about the lack of women in science and fought for better recognition of the sciences in her native Italy. When she celebrated her hundredth birthday some 20 years later, she received the honour of being the oldest ever Nobel Prize winner. "I am not afraid of death – I am privileged to have been able to work for so long," she said. "If I die tomorrow or in a year, it is the same – it is the message you leave behind you that counts, and the young scientists who carry on your work."[21]

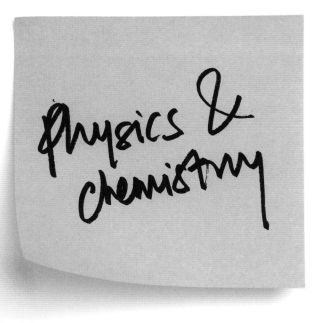

hen **Chien-Shiung Wu** (1912–1997) was a student at the prestigious Suzhou Girls' High School in the Chinese city of Suzhou, she encountered a biography of Marie Curie, the great chemist and physicist who became the first woman to win a Nobel Prize and the only woman to win it twice. Curie's achievements ignited a lifelong passion in a teenager who was already so devoted to science that she spent her free time teaching herself physics from textbooks borrowed from friends. But Wu probably never imagined that she would grow up to be a scientific pioneer just like her hero, or that her contributions would earn her the nickname "the Chinese Madame Curie".

Born in 1912 to two politically progressive parents, Wu came to symbolize their hopes for the future of the country. With the overthrow of the weak and corrupt Qing dynasty and the inauguration of the Republic of China, her parents saw an opportunity to challenge the long-held prejudice against women's education. They founded the Mingde School for Girls together, with Wu's father taking on the job of principal and her mother tasked with persuading families in the region to enrol their daughters. Wu was one of their first students, and she whizzed through the elementary grades on offer and left home at the age of 10 or 11 to continue her education at Suzhou Girls' High, some 50 miles away from her birthplace of Liuhe. Her grades in high school were so impressive that she was immediately offered a place at the National Central University in Nanjing, the usual entrance examination requirement having been waived.

By the time she graduated with top marks in 1934, her chosen subject of physics had become one of the liveliest and most exciting disciplines in the world: breakthroughs like Albert Einstein's theory of relativity had revolutionized the field and each year promised ever more astounding discoveries. But China had no graduate programme for aspiring physicists and she quickly realized that she would have to fly the nest to pursue her dream. In August 1936, she waved goodbye to her family and friends from the *President Hoover* ocean liner, bound for the distant shores of America.

It was the last time she saw her mother and father. After switching from the University of Michigan to the University of California, Berkeley, Wu immersed herself in her graduate degree, only to receive news a year in that Japan had invaded China. She didn't hear from her parents for eight years and the conflict between the two nations would later merge into the Second World War with the bombing of Pearl Harbor in 1941.

Wu was extremely worried about her family, but work provided a much-needed distraction. She carved out a reputation as a meticulous and dogged experimental physicist of the highest calibre. When future Nobel Prize winner Enrico Fermi had trouble with his experiments, he was told to call on Wu. Among physicists, the saying went: "If the experiment was done by Wu, it must be correct."[1] In his autobiography, her mentor Emilio Segrè recalled: "Wu's will power and devotion to work are reminiscent of Marie Curie, but she is more worldly, elegant, and witty."[2]

In 1944, Wu was invited to join the top-secret Manhattan Project under the auspices of her former professor, Robert Oppenheimer, to work on crucial problems including uranium enrichment and radiation detection at Columbia University. She was the only Chinese person to work in the war department and one of the only women among its senior researchers. In 1945, she saw the culmination of her efforts with the development of the atomic bomb. Though she later expressed regret over its use on Hiroshima and Nagasaki, the work that she did helped to usher the Second World War to a much earlier close and allowed her to finally receive word that her family was safe. She expressed the hope that the devastating bomb was a one-off: "Do you think that people are so stupid and self-destructive? No. I have confidence in humankind. I believe we will one day live together peacefully."[3]

When the war ended, Wu stayed on at Columbia University to teach and continue her research into beta decay, a radioactive process in which the nucleus of an atom emits beta particles, forcing the atom to change into a new element. Nobody actually knew how beta decay worked and Wu was on the cutting edge of this new science. Her expertise brought her to the attention of Tsung-Dao Lee and Chen-Ning Yang, two scientists who were investigating a law in physics known as the conservation of parity. It was believed that fundamental symmetry governed everything in nature, including the behaviour of atomic particles. But Lee and Yang theorized that parity might not exist with beta decay; they just needed someone to prove it.

Enter Wu. Using super-cooled radioactive cobalt, she devised a series of experiments that later proved this so-called fundamental law of science wrong. If the law of parity was true, the cobalt nuclei would break down and jettison the same number of electrons in symmetrical directions. After months of operating on only a few hours of sleep a night – she even cancelled a long-awaited return visit to China – Wu was able to prove that this wasn't the case. The explosive news landed Wu on the cover of the *New York Times*. "We learn one lesson," she later said, "never accept any 'self-evident' principle."[4]

Lee and Yang were later awarded the Nobel Prize in Physics in 1954, but Wu's efforts in proving their theory right went unacknowledged. "Although I did not do research just for the prize, it still hurts me a lot that my work was overlooked for certain reasons," she wrote to Jack Steinberger, a fellow physicist who steadfastly maintained that Wu should have shared in the Nobel triumph.[5] She was decorated with honours in every other way, including the National Medal of Science and the Wolf Prize in Physics (the latter is considered the second most prestigious award in the sciences, after the Nobel Prize). She even had an asteroid named after her in 1990. But as she told a biographer, the glory of scientific discovery was its own award. "These are moments of exaltation and ecstasy," she said of her findings about parity. "A glimpse of this wonder can be the reward of a lifetime."[6]

ne July morning in 1938, **Lise Meitner** (1878–1968) boarded the train that would take her out of Germany and into Holland. She had only ten marks in her pocket and carried two small suitcases that she had hastily packed. The only thing of value that she had was a diamond ring that her "colleague-brother"[7], the chemist Otto Hahn, had given her: it was his mother's heirloom, to be pawned or traded in case of emergency. Meitner was fleeing the Nazis.

"I have left Germany forever," the physicist mused in a letter to a friend.[8] Adolf Hitler's diabolical rise to power meant that Jewish people in Germany were in grave danger, and that also included Austrian Jews, even those who had converted to Protestantism, as Meitner had in 1908. At the Kaiser Wilhelm Institute for Chemistry, whispers were growing about the "Jewess" undertaking research into radioactivity.

When it looked increasingly likely that she might be dismissed from the Institute as part of a purge of German universities, she tentatively applied for permission to leave the country. It was rejected. According to the Ministry of the Interior, it was "undesirable that well-known Jews leave Germany to travel abroad where they appear to be representatives of German science".[9] Meitner knew then that she had to run. After her academic colleagues successfully smuggled her out over the border, she ended up in Stockholm, forced to start a new life at the age of 60.

It wasn't meant to be like this. Born into a middle-class Viennese family in 1878, Meitner grew up in the circle of writers, lawyers and intellectuals inhabited by her smart, upwardly mobile parents. At a time when most European universities were barred to women, she was one of only four girls who passed the Matura, an entrance examination for the University of Vienna. Still, the thought of further study was difficult to grasp: "I was very uneasy in my mind as to whether I would be able to become a scientist," she said later. "So I also took my teaching diploma and did my year's trial at a girls' high school, in order to keep these possibilities open."[10]

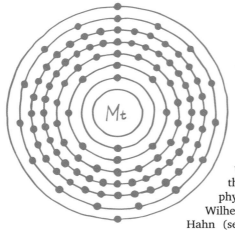

Thankfully, Meitner's aptitude for science was clear to everyone around her. Armed with a doctorate in physics – the discipline that "brought light and fullness into my life",[11] as she put it – she was able to travel to Berlin in 1907 to study under the renowned German theoretical physicist Max Planck at the Friedrich-Wilhelms-Universität, where she met Hahn (see page 119). She brought her intimate knowledge of physics to his chemistry know-how and they began researching the emerging field of radioactivity together, although Meitner had to work in the basement for a year before the university department allowed women into its labs. As the decades wore on, she was chosen to lead the physics department of the Kaiser Wilhelm Institute for Chemistry and grew closer to Hahn as a friend and colleague. The First World War interrupted their research when Hahn was called up for military service and Meitner volunteered as a nurse, but the two tried to take their periods of leave together so they could continue their work in Berlin.

This fruitful partnership would see its culmination in the discovery of nuclear fission, a scientific landmark that would lead to Hahn, but not Meitner, receiving the Nobel Prize in Chemistry in 1944.

By the time Meitner sought refuge in Sweden, she had spent years on an investigation into uranium, the heaviest naturally occurring element on earth. She persuaded Hahn to join her on the project and together they bombarded uranium with neutrons to see if they could artificially create even heavier elements. They were up against the clock; several leading physicists and chemists, including Irène and Frédéric Joliot-Curie, were trying to discover these so-called transuranium elements.

Unfortunately, the Nazi threat in Germany effectively put an end to Meitner and Hahn's lab partnership, though they began exchanging letters in an attempt to work on the uranium problem long distance.

As Meitner struggled to find her feet in Stockholm, Hahn continued working with German scientist Fritz Strassmann on Meitner's investigation, though the two chemists were somewhat hampered by their lack of physics experience.

In December 1938, Hahn wrote to her about a "frightful conclusion"[12] that he and Strassmann had encountered during their experiments: instead of creating even heavier elements, colliding neutrons with uranium had produced smaller ones. "Perhaps you can come up with some fantastic explanation," he pleaded, adding in another letter, "If there is anything you could propose that you could publish, then it would still in a way be work by the three of us!"[13]

During a bracing Christmas-time walk through the snow, Meitner and her visiting nephew and physicist Otto Robert Frisch teased out the theory of nuclear fission for the first time. What if, they mused, firing neutrons at the nucleus of uranium wasn't producing heavier elements, but rather it was splitting the atom into smaller parts and expending huge amounts of energy while doing it? Forget the transuranics: this was nuclear fission at work!

Though Strassmann would later describe Meitner as the "intellectual leader of our team",[14] Hahn claimed full credit for this discovery. As far as he was concerned, it was irrelevant that the uranium project was Meitner's idea to begin with and that she had helped him puzzle out the mysterious results in his lab. In 1944 Hahn was named the sole recipient of the Nobel Prize in Chemistry, though, as Meitner put it:

"Surely Hahn fully deserved the Nobel Prize for chemistry. There is really no doubt about it. But I believe that Otto Robert Frisch and I contributed something not insignificant to the clarification of the process of uranium fission – how it originates and that it produces so much energy and that was something very remote to Hahn."[15]

When the records of the Nobel Prize committee were unsealed in the 1990s, historians like Ruth Lewin Sime excavated the true extent to which Meitner had been overlooked in the Nobel judgment. In 1997 she was rewarded for her contributions to science with her own element: meitnerium, with a half-life of just a few seconds.

eona Woods Marshall Libby (1919–1986) looks out of the black-and-white photograph from underneath a thick mop of dark hair, a slight grin on her lips. It was 2 December 1946. Libby and her colleagues had plenty to smile about: they were celebrating the fourth anniversary of their world-changing achievement. They were the people behind the world's first self-sustained nuclear fission reaction, led by the Italian physicist Enrico Fermi, and Libby was the only woman and the youngest member of the team.

The momentous day took place in secret, in the less than impressive surroundings of a squash court sunk beneath the stands of the University of Chicago's football field. The world's first nuclear reactor was tiny by modern-day standards; only 2.4 metres (8 feet) long and 3.4 metres (11 feet) tall, it was made from graphite bricks and timber, and powered by uranium. Chicago Pile-1 (or CP-1 for short) paved the way for the end of the Second World War and it couldn't have happened without Libby's help.

Born in 1919, Libby grew up in suburban Illinois and studied chemistry at the University of Chicago, specializing in molecular spectroscopy. Her expertise brought her to the attention of the Manhattan Project (see also page 130), which was competing with Nazi Germany to develop the first atomic bomb after the discovery of nuclear fission in 1938 (see page 135) cracked open the possibility of nuclear weapons. The Manhattan Project needed someone well versed in molecular behaviour to join the top-secret Chicago Metallurgical Laboratory to build detectors that tracked the nuclear reaction. Libby – a brilliant doctoral student – was the best person for the job. She was only 23.

When CP-1 went critical, it was Libby's instruments that determined that the experiment was a success, even if it created only about half a watt of energy, which is not enough to light up an average light bulb. The team marked the occasion with a small bottle of Chianti (Italian, just like their leader Fermi) decanted into paper cups. "[We] passed them around in the midst of that dingy, gray-black surrounding without any word whatsoever. No toast, nothing, and everyone had a few memorable sips,"[16] she recalled. One by one, they signed the label of the wine bottle to commemorate the day.

CP-1 was dismantled and rebuilt at a more remote location, while Libby continued to work on other nuclear piles. She was so committed that she was still working two days before she went into labour with her son, Peter, and promptly returned a week after his birth. (She kept the bump hidden underneath a pair of overalls and a blue denim jacket, and would arrive at the reactor just in time to vomit from morning sickness before beginning her day.)

Libby and her husband, John Marshall Jr, worked together to construct other nuclear reactors at Hanford in Washington State, which were crucial for producing the plutonium for bombs. Once again, she was one of the only women at the centre of the action. Women were such a rare sight in the production plant that Libby had to have a private toilet built for her on-site.

The Manhattan Project culminated in the creation of the first atomic bomb and its deployment on the Japanese cities of Hiroshima and Nagasaki. While other scientists who worked on the bomb, such as Chien-Shiung Wu (see page 128), expressed regret that their contributions to nuclear fission had led to the death of thousands of people, Libby was more pragmatic; the bombings, she maintained, were necessary for an immediate end to the Second World War. "I certainly do recall how I felt when the atomic bombs were used," she said later. "My brother-in-law was captain of the first minesweeper scheduled into Sasebo Harbor...It was pretty clear the war would continue [otherwise], with half a million of our fighting men dead, not to say how many Japanese."[17]

After the bombings of Hiroshima and Nagasaki, Japan surrendered to the Allies, ushering in the end of the war. Libby returned to the University of Chicago to work with Fermi at the Institute for Nuclear Studies. When her old mentor died in 1954, she took up fellowships at institutions such as New York University and the University of California, Los Angeles, and published more than 200 scientific papers, including the autobiographical book *The Uranium People* (1979), which documented the behind-the-scenes history of the atom bomb. She also became an outspoken advocate for nuclear power and never lost faith that the Manhattan Project changed the course of history for the better, even if it was at an enormous cost: "If the Germans had got [the bomb] before we did, I don't know what would have happened to the world," she said. "I have no regrets. I think we did right, and we couldn't have done it differently."[18]

he history of women in science doesn't just go back to tales of female scientists and philosophers such as Hypatia of Alexandria (see page 152); it also extends some 6,000 years back to ancient empires in Mesopotamia, the cradle of civilization. Many of these women's names have since been lost in time and all that remains of them are depictions of their likenesses in stone carvings. But one of the first women whose name we do know belongs to that of a Babylonian chemist:

Tapputi-Belatekallim (c.1200 BC)

Archaeologists found a record of her work in clay cuneiform texts dating back to 1200 BC. In ancient Babylon, perfumes were not just cosmetic scents for beauty purposes: they were fragranced substances that were required for medicinal purposes and religious rituals alike. As a royal perfume-maker, Tapputi wasn't just the head of her own household (which is what "Belatekallim" means); she is spoken of as being an authority in her field and the official overseer of perfumery in the royal palace.

As any modern-day perfumer will tell you, the creation of perfumes – even for cosmetic reasons alone – doesn't just entail mixing up scents to see what smells nicest. It requires an intimate knowledge of chemistry and an understanding of technical processes such as extraction and sublimation. Tapputi wielded these skills well over a millennia ago.

We know little of Tapputi's background or personal life, but history has left us with one of her recipes: a fragrant salve for the Babylonian king. In this fascinating relic, Tapputi takes the reader through the step-by-step routine necessary to produce a royal ointment containing, water, flowers, oil and calamus, which may either refer to lemongrass or a reed-like plant that is still used in perfumes today. She describes the process of refining the ingredients in her 'still': a chemical apparatus for distilling and filtering liquids. Advanced versions of such equipment remain in use in labs today, but Tapputi's reference to a still is the oldest in human history. That makes her one of the earliest chemical engineers that we know of.

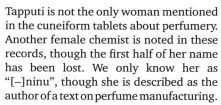

Tapputi is not the only woman mentioned in the cuneiform tablets about perfumery. Another female chemist is noted in these records, though the first half of her name has been lost. We only know her as "[–]ninu", though she is described as the author of a text on perfume manufacturing.

It's not surprising that women were so intimately involved with chemistry. The list of equipment used seems to be co-opted straight from a Babylonian kitchen or adapted and modified from everyday utensils and cookware. This appears to suggest that women were chemistry's earliest adopters and innovators, and that there is a lot less separating the art of cuisine from the science of chemistry than many people may think.

efore **Laura Bassi** (1711–1778) turned 21, the streets of her native Bologna, Italy, were awash with talk of the polymath who could speak flawless Latin and expound on Cartesian and Newtonian logic. She was duly summoned to present herself and argue her case before a council of curious intellectuals, including five University of Bologna academics and the future Pope Benedict XIV. They were so dazzled by her performance that they awarded the young woman with a doctorate in philosophy and appointed her as a university chair a few months afterward.

It was a pretty remarkable feat for a woman of her age. What was even more astounding was that it happened in 1732, exactly 213 years before women got the vote in Italy. The liberal city of Bologna had always prided itself on its intellectually progressive history and now it hailed Bassi as its most extraordinary daughter. A silver crown of laurels was placed on her head during her degree ceremony, and a bronze medal bearing her image and comparing her to Minerva, the goddess of wisdom, was stamped in her honour. The attendance list of her award ceremony and her inaugural lecture reads like a Who's Who of Bolognese society, including the archbishop of the city, government senators and noble dignitaries. "All the gentlemen of Bologna make a great display of this girl, and depict her everywhere as the miracle of our age," wrote the Italian scientist Giovanni Bianchi.[19]

Born to a lawyer and his sickly wife in 1711, Bassi demonstrated an early aptitude for Latin and sought refuge in her father's books. The Bassi family doctor was so taken with her obvious intelligence that he began teaching her philosophy free of charge. As the years passed, the young Laura could be found in fierce intellectual debate with visiting scholars in the privacy of the Bassi home.

When the University of Bologna awarded her the doctorate, she was only the second woman in history to gain a degree and subsequently Europe's first female professor in experimental physics (or, as she called it, "la nostra Fisica"[20]).

Word of her genius soon spread across Europe, with Voltaire sending her letters begging her to help him get into the Bolognese Academy of Sciences:

"I have been wishing to journey to Bologna in order to be able one day to tell my countrymen I have seen Signora Bassi... There is no Bassi in London, and I would be much happier to be added to your Academy of Bologna than to that of the English, even though it has produced a Newton."[21]

Of course, 18th-century Europe was still no haven for a woman scientist, no matter how well she could speak Latin or hold forth on Sir Isaac Newton's new and exciting theories of natural philosophy. Bassi was not allowed to lecture at the university as frequently as her male peers; the governing board asked her to give a lecture three times a year "by reason of sex".[22] Although her peers fêted her as the "new light of philosophy" and the "luminous mirror of Science",[23] she understandably felt compelled to strike out on her own.

After marrying her fellow professor Giuseppe Veratti – a man she once sweetly described in a letter as "a person who walks the same path of learning, and who, from long experience, I was certain would not dissuade me from it"[24] – she set about transforming their house on Via Barberia into a laboratory where she could conduct Newton-influenced experiments on electricity and light. In 1749 Bassi began a private school in her own home, where aspiring scientists could combine experimental study with a more traditional framework of natural philosophy. Its unique programme was unlike anything else on offer in Bologna and students from all over Europe soon came knocking on her door.

In a letter to a friend in 1755 she mused:

"It is six years since I began giving private physics classes in my house daily, for eight months of the year...I support these myself, paying for all the necessary equipment apart from that which my husband had made when he was lecturing in philosophy. The classes have gathered such momentum that they are now attended by people of considerable education, including foreigners, rather than by youths."[25]

Unfortunately, little remains of Bassi's scientific work: she did not publish many research papers, and there is scant documentation of her public lectures and private classes. But her greatest achievement could be seen in her influence on her students, many of whom went on to become physicists themselves. "In our time," she proclaimed, "experimental physics has become such a useful and necessary science".[26] A large part of this was down to Bassi herself.

orothy Hodgkin (1910–1994) was just 10 when her teacher showed her how to mix copper sulphate and alum. Over the next few days, she was hypnotized by the sight of glittering crystals forming in the solution. "I was captured for life by chemistry and by crystals," she later said.[27]

This basic science experiment is performed by thousands of schoolchildren every year, but few of them go on to become Nobel-Prize-winning scientists. When UNESCO designated 2014 as the International Year of Crystallography, few people outside the field of biochemistry understood what the term "crystallography" meant, or why it was important enough to merit its own centenary year. But X-ray crystallography has been responsible for some of the greatest scientific revelations of the 20th century, including the discovery of DNA in 1953, and nobody wielded this dark art better than Hodgkin.

Hodgkin was only a child when Max von Laue and father–son duo William and Lawrence Bragg consecutively won the Nobel Prize (in 1914 and 1915) for pioneering the scientific technique that would bring us one step closer to understanding the atomic structure of all matter on earth. These men had found that passing X-ray beams through a crystal created a distinctive pattern of spots on a photographic plate, enabling them to see that each crystal was made of a three-dimensional lattice of atoms. The discovery had dramatic implications: if scientists could induce a substance to crystallize, they could conceivably use X-ray crystallography to tease out the invisible arrangements of atoms that held it together.

Her father was determined that Dorothy – the eldest of three daughters – should receive the same education as a firstborn son, and she didn't let him down. At Somerville College, Oxford, she even spent her twenty-first birthday in the labs deep in study; when people begged her to put down her books and have some fun, her standard response was, "Don't you understand, I've got to know!"[28] She was introduced to X-ray crystallography for the first time at Somerville and travelled to Germany to study under renowned crystallographer Victor Goldschmidt, who was such a devotee of his subject that he had written "Crystallography is the Queen of the Sciences" on the walls of his lab.

By the time Somerville awarded Hodgkin a research fellowship in 1933, scientists were beginning to use X-ray crystallography to unravel the inner makings of biological molecules: a daunting and complex task. When she received a rare sample of crystallized insulin, she took a year to work out a recipe to make them large enough for photographic analysis. When she finally managed to take a picture of insulin after a late night in the lab, she wandered through Oxford in a joyful daze. Hodgkin published an article in *Nature* just a month before her twenty-fifth birthday.

X-ray crystallography wasn't as straightforward as just coaxing the growth of crystals and photographing them. For every picture, Hodgkin had to undertake huge amounts of calculations to work out if the diffraction pattern in the image matched up to her hypothesis of the molecule's atomic structure. Bigger molecules demanded even more arduous and time-consuming mathematical work, and Hodgkin was working long before the advent of the personal computer. It often took her years to disentangle complicated proteins and molecules; she spent more than three decades attempting to tease out the atomic structure of insulin alone.

Hodgkin was a well-loved professor at Oxford – former student Margaret Thatcher, who disagreed with her left-wing pacifist teacher on pretty much everything, nonetheless respected her so much that she apparently

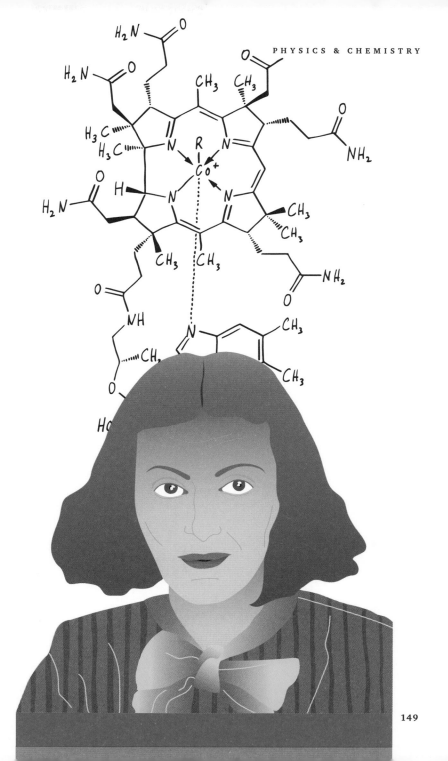

kept a picture of Hodgkin at 10 Downing Street, London – but her findings weren't always welcomed by the scientific establishment. When she cracked the structure of penicillin in 1945, a chemist named John Cornforth reportedly declared, "If that's the formula of penicillin, I'll give up chemistry and grow mushrooms."[29]

Hodgkin was right, of course, and while Cornforth didn't leave science to farm mushrooms, her discovery did pave the way for the creation of semi-synthetic penicillin, which can be chemically modified for specific treatments and forms the basis of many life saving antibiotics. To this day, Hodgkin's breakthroughs continue to affect the lives of millions of people around the world, not least when she finally puzzled out the structure of insulin in 1969, just one year short of turning 60.

In 1964, Hodgkin was awarded the Nobel Prize for her discoveries of the structure of penicillin and vitamin B12. At the prize-giving ceremony in Stockholm, Hodgkin displayed her characteristic humility and warm sense of humour: "I should not like to leave an impression that all structural problems can be settled by X-ray analysis or that all crystal structures are easy to solve," she said in her Nobel lecture. "I seem to have spent much more of my life not solving structures than solving them."[30]

Mathematics

lexandria, the great Mediterranean city believed to have been founded by Alexander the Great around 331 BC, was home to between 300,000 and a million people of all faiths and backgrounds[1]: Christians, Jews and pagans lived and worked in its thriving ports, markets and temples. It was also the birthplace of one of antiquity's most extraordinary – and most tragic – philosophers and mathematicians.

Hypatia of Alexandria (c.AD 355) was born into the elite ranks of Alexandria's upper class; her father was Theon, a prominent public intellectual and the head of a school of philosophy. At the time, most upper-class women finished their schooling in their late teens, as soon as they married, but Hypatia must have demonstrated a knack for learning early on. Theon tutored her when she was a child and she quickly "far surpassed her teacher".[2] She soon graduated from private tuition to attending lessons at Theon's school and then moved on to teaching at the institution herself, eventually taking over her father's position.

Under Hypatia's lead, the school began to teach an inventive and sophisticated blend of mathematics and Platonic philosophy, attracting scholars from all corners of the Roman empire. She was adored by her students and respected by the people of Alexandria. In her traditional philosopher's cloak, she would hold forth on Plato and Aristotle in lectures that were open to the public, which was in sharp contrast to the exclusivity and closed halls of other schools. The *Suda*, a 10th-century dictionary and encyclopedia, notes that she was "both skilful and eloquent in words and prudent and civil in deeds", "loved and honoured... exceptionally" by all who encountered her.[3]

Hypatia was so devoted to academia that she is thought to have spurned marriage, preferring books and celibacy to married life. In accordance with philosophical principles, Hypatia and her students nurtured a strictly non-sexual love for each other, bound by intellect and love of the divine.

On one occasion, however, a student was struck with lust for Hypatia and confessed his love for her. When she failed to put him off, she showed the would-be philosopher a menstrual rag and declared: "It is this that you love, not something beautiful."[4] It was her way of reminding him of the baseness of the human body, far removed from the sanctity of the mind; sufficiently rebuked, the student turned away and forgot his lust.

But as Hypatia grew into an esteemed intellectual, her birthplace was also changing beyond recognition. The balance of power in the bustling metropolis was beginning to favour the Christian faith: traditional religious practices such as night sacrifices were banned, and pagan temples and shrines to the east were ransacked and destroyed. These religious divisions worsened in AD 385, when a young bishop named Theophilus became patriarch of the city and religious leader of its booming Christian population.

Theophilus openly mocked Alexandria's pagans; when an old shrine was discovered, he laughingly paraded its religious symbols through the city as a joke. As a full-blown riot broke out, a pagan mob seized Christian prisoners and retreated to the Serapeum, an enormous temple to the Greco-Egyptian god Serapis. Just as the emperor threatened a military siege, the pagan occupiers fled in panic, only to see a horde of Christians ransack their temple and pull down its statue.

The patriarch set Alexandria on a dangerous course with his actions, and his successor and nephew, Cyril, came to power with no reservations about threatening enemies of his faith with violence. Alexandria's governor, Orestes, desperately needed to find a mediator and wise counsellor who could defuse the tensions in the city. This duty fell to Hypatia – and would have devastating consequences.

In many ways, Hypatia was a perfect candidate for soothing the fraying tempers in the city. She was a pagan, but practised a form of philosophy that encouraged contemplation of the divine through intellectual activity, not via the traditional rituals preached by other philosophers. Her school of thought was neither pagan nor Christian; it trod a fine line between the two. In fact, her teachings drew many Christians to her school, who happily sat alongside their pagan brothers in classes.

As Hypatia and Orestes attempted to find a way to reconcile the warring communities, Cyril's supporters grew convinced that Hypatia had enchanted the governor and was engineering a plot against their leader. In the spring of AD 415, a group of Christians led by a church official named Peter approached her house, probably intending to intimidate her and drive her away from Orestes.

Instead, fate conspired to have the mob encounter Hypatia in public. Fuelled by rage and paranoia, they dragged her through the streets and stripped her naked; her body was hacked apart with broken tiles and her remains set alight. It was a gruesome end to one of antiquity's greatest philosophers and mathematicians, and an especially horrifying one for someone whose school embodied the tolerance and mutual respect that could exist between pagans and Christians.

Sadly, her untimely demise meant that she left behind no successor. The unique school founded by one of the greatest mathematicians in the Greco-Roman world was left in ruins.

f history were kinder to the fairer sex, Paris-born **Émilie du Châtelet** (1706–1749) would go down as one of the Enlightenment's most brilliant polymaths. Instead, she is more often remembered as one of Voltaire's lovers, and while the playwright, philosopher and writer is saluted as one of the 18th century's greatest minds, it is likely he would have been more than a little disappointed not to find Du Châtelet on the list with him.

The Marquise du Châtelet was a formidable author, scientist and mathematician: a true *femme savant*. But she was also no high-society female confined indoors; she conducted torrid love affairs, went to glamorous parties, collected Meissen porcelain and fanciful snuffboxes, dressed in fine ermine and marten-trimmed gowns,[5] and gambled with other aristocrats, shocking them with her impressive ability to carry out speedy mental calculations. (She used the profits to purchase scientific equipment and books.) To Voltaire's astonishment, she once divided a nine-figure number by nine other figures in her head. He shouldn't have been surprised; after all, this was the woman who had learned to speak six languages by the time she was twelve.

Du Châtelet's greatest achievement, however, lay in her translation of Sir Isaac Newton's *Principia* (1687), the revolutionary text that introduced the laws of motion and gravity to the world. Du Châtelet was born 19 years after Newton published his seminal work in Latin, but France was still in thrall to Cartesian science by the time she grew up and began her studies. She laboured harder than anyone to bring Newton's ideas to the public, producing the first French translation and commentary on *Principia* in 1759, which remains the standard text in the country today. It was no easy feat to translate Newton into French, but Du Châtelet excelled at the task, finding ways to express his complicated proofs in elegant, accessible language. In combining Anglo-Dutch research with the work of German mathematician Gottfried Leibniz, some believe that she also laid the foundations for Albert Einstein to come up with the equation $E=mc^2$ a century or so later.

Du Châtelet's accomplishments were all the more startling given the lack of opportunities for women of her rank. Her father was unusual in encouraging his child's interest in education and books, hiring tutors for his gifted daughter and disregarding her mother's suggestion of sending the unruly girl to a convent. He even helped to arrange a suitable marriage to the Marquis du Chastellet-Lomont, an older army officer who was, conveniently, often away for battle.

As an adult, Du Châtelet resourcefully sought some of France's best tutors and scholars to mentor her in mathematics, and wasn't averse to flouting convention in her quest for knowledge, too. On one occasion, Café Gradot, a Paris watering hole for men to gather for intellectual discussion, politely ejected her when she attempted to join one of her teachers. Undeterred, she simply had some men's clothing made and strolled back in drag.

At a time when most women were not expected to expend much energy on intellectual pursuits, Du Châtelet argued for all to receive the education that she herself had pursued so tenaciously. In the preface for her translation of Bernard Mandeville's *The Fable of the Bees* (1714), she wrote passionately:

"I confess that if I were king, I would conduct the following experiment…I would get women to participate in all the privileges of humanity, especially those of the mind. It's as though women were born only to flirt, so they are given nothing but that activity to exercise their minds. The new education I propose would do all of humanity a great deal of good. Women would be better off for it, and men would gain a new source of competition."[6]

When she and Voltaire fell in love, it was both romantic and intellectual. (Like a true Frenchman, Du Châtelet's husband was supremely unbothered by the affair, even when the pair of lovers moved to Cirey, a country estate that he owned in eastern France.)

At Cirey, both of them plunged into their work, transforming the house into a place of research. They stacked its shelves with more than 20,000 books and built a laboratory in its corridors. Du Châtelet was devoted to the pursuit of science; if she had trouble staying up all night to work, she would simply sink her hands into iced water to jolt herself awake.

Voltaire both admired and respected her ferocious intellect, explicitly acknowledging her contributions in the *Elements of the Philosophy of Newton*: she appears as a radiant muse in the frontispiece for the 1738 book, reflecting the light of Newton's discoveries onto Voltaire, who is depicted writing at his desk. Two years later, however, she had well surpassed the role; her book, *Institutions de Physique* (1740), was translated into German shortly after its publication and was later cited by philosopher Immanuel Kant.[7]

Voltaire and Du Châtelet lived together for 15 years, but when the relationship fizzled out, she took on a young poet as a lover at the age of 42. Du Châtelet, a master at dealing with difficult social as well as scientific proofs, was able to remain friends with her former lover. But her new love affair ended in unexpected pregnancy. She began fearing that she might not survive childbirth – few women of her age did – despite still slaving over her magnum opus, the translation of *Principia*.

Du Châtelet intensified her work on her book, finishing it at the end of August, but she was still at her writing desk even when she gave birth in September (Voltaire wrote that the baby daughter was temporarily laid on a geometry book). It seemed, at least for the moment, that her sense of foreboding was misplaced. But a week later, Du Châtelet suddenly passed away, and the child soon followed. Voltaire, on the other hand, lived to 83 and secured his reputation as one of the Enlightenment's most famous minds.

As for Du Châtelet, she is only now shaking off her reputation as Voltaire's favourite mistress. It's lucky that she has Newton – and the law of gravity – on her side.

ntil the 1970s, most people thought that Bletchley Park was just a run-of-the-mill stately home in suburban Buckinghamshire, UK. But when former MI6 officer F W Winterbotham wrote an explosive tell-all titled *The Ultra Secret* (1974), the code-breaking operation stationed at this unassuming country estate was exposed. During the tail end of the Second World War, thousands of people were stationed at Bletchley and tasked with cracking the secret communications of the Axis powers.

Essayist and scholar George Steiner once described Bletchley as "the single greatest achievement of Britain during 1939–45, perhaps during the [20th] century as a whole."[8] It is even believed that the efforts of those at Bletchley shortened the war by two years. What everyone forgets, however, is that the majority of people at Bletchley were women.

Today, Bletchley Park is better remembered as the home of the computing genius Alan Turing, and films like *The Imitation Game* (2014) imply that the war on German intelligence was won mainly by a small circle of gifted male mathematicians. In truth, there were some 9,000 people working at Bletchley by the end of the war and three-quarters of them were women. Over a period of four years, the code-breakers toiled away in cramped wooden huts to mine enemy communications for anything that might give Britain the advantage over its enemies.

These dedicated women have come to be known as **The Bletchleyettes**; back then, they were simply known to the male employees as "the girls". They were mostly young and educated women recruited from schools, universities, department stores and banks to assist in the war effort. Some were only 15 years old, having lied about their age during the enlistment process. Several had degrees in mathematics or foreign languages such as German and Japanese; others had been pulled from secretarial colleges.

In nearby hostels and rooms rented in local homes, upper-class debutantes shared sleeping quarters with East End girls and were bused into "Station X" every day. All of them had signed the Official Secrets Act and were sworn to lifelong secrecy; as former decoder Rozanne Colchester put it: "You were told that if you talked about it, you could be shot. It was all terribly exciting."[9]

The Park's leading team of female code-breakers, known as Dilly's Girls, was assembled at the request of Dillwyn "Dilly" Knox, an eccentric academic whose motto was "nothing is impossible". "He was sat by the window wreathed in smoke," recalls Mavis Lever of her first encounter with him. "He said: 'Hello. Have you got a pencil? We're breaking machines.'"[10]

Lever would go on to crack a message link between Belgrade and Berlin, a breakthrough that would later pave the way to unlock the communications of the German secret service. The mathematician Margaret Rock also joined Lever's team; together, the two women formed an indomitable pair and served as an inspiration to the other women in the team. Dilly once boasted about his all-star group: "Give me a Rock and a Lever and I can move the universe."[11]

Dilly's Girls went on to hand the Royal Navy one of its greatest victories in the war, when Lever cracked an Italian Navy message that simply read: "Today's the day minus three." They worked through three complete days and nights, pausing only to take short naps and grab quick bites of food.

Thanks to their work, the British fleet was able to surprise the enemy off the Greek coast, sinking three Italian heavy cruisers and two destroyers.

As victory dawned in the Mediterranean, a British admiral sent a grateful message to Bletchley Park: "Tell Dilly, we have won a great victory...and it's all thanks to him and his girls."[12]

Rock and Lever were not the only women to excel at Bletchley Park. Joan Clarke was assigned to Turing's team after being recruited by her Cambridge professor, becoming one of the first senior female cryptanalysts at the Park. There was little to no protocol for a woman to ascend to this rank. Instead, Clarke was classed as a linguist and the mathematics graduate took extra glee in marking "grade: linguist, languages: none" on official forms.[13]

Despite their best efforts, the women struggled to get the same pay and opportunities as their male peers. The men in Clarke's hut, for instance, were still on a higher salary even after she was promoted to deputy head. This inequality applied to all the women who made up the ranks of clerks, bomb operators and other technical jobs that received and transmitted the secret communications that oiled the British war machine.

As soon as the war ended, the women were ejected into regular society and expected to go back to being housewives. "We all heard stories of the young mothers with good brains who suddenly found they had a husband at work all day and two small children at home and went nearly batty with frustration," one female code-breaker explained. "It was a quite severe social problem after the war."[14]

In 2009 the Government Communications Headquarters (GCHQ) finally recognized the contributions of the Bletchleyettes by awarding female veterans with gold 'We Also Served' badges. A remote station listener named Betty Gilbert recently went to Bletchley to receive her salutation and award. "I always said, 'All I want is a thank you for what I did,'" she commented. "They couldn't have done it without us, and finally I've got that thank you!"[15]

n 1916 the German-born physicist Albert Einstein published his groundbreaking paper on the general theory of relativity. At the University of Göttingen in Germany, a 34-year-old mathematician by the name of **Emmy Noether** (1882–1935) read Einstein's work with great interest and began to apply her prodigious mind to the wider complexities of his theory. Einstein was impressed by the results: "It would not have done the Old Guard at Göttingen any harm had they picked up a thing or two from her," he wrote. "She certainly knows what she is doing."[16]

Emmy's resulting theory is known as Noether's theorem. It is now taught on university campuses all over the world, and some scientists believe it to be just as important as the theory of relativity. Noether herself has been described by *New York Times* as the "mighty mathematician you've never heard of". Through published work and lectures well-attended by eager students, she essentially created abstract algebra: a relatively young field of study that uses algebraic structures, such as groups, vector spaces and rings, rather than numbers.

You might think this would be enough to transform Noether into the mathematics equivalent of a celebrity. Despite her groundbreaking work and the love and respect of her immediate colleagues, Noether was 41 by the time the university administrators finally awarded her with the official title of *nicht beamteter ausserordentlicher* professor; essentially, she was the equivalent of a lowly tenured research assistant. The post was also unpaid.

One Göttingen co-worker tried in vain to fight her corner. "I was ashamed to occupy such a preferred position beside her whom I knew to be my superior as a mathematician in many respects," the mathematician Hermann Weyl once said. "Tradition, prejudice, external considerations weighted the balance against her scientific merits and scientific greatness, by that time denied by no one."[17]

To her credit, Noether was already a trailblazer in university education by the time she arrived at Göttingen. As the oldest daughter in a middle-class Jewish family residing in Erlangen, a town in southern Germany, Noether had qualified as a language teacher in 1900 when she heard that women were finally allowed to go to lectures at the local university, though they could not matriculate. Just two years previously, the Academic Senate at Erlangen had pronounced that letting women on campus would "overthrow all academic order",[18] but Noether was undeterred. Once women were allowed to sit examinations alongside men, she went on to receive a doctorate at Erlangen and began teaching and supervising students.

By the time leading mathematician David Hilbert invited Noether to join his team at Göttingen, she had been toiling away in Erlangen unpaid for seven years. But the university refused Hilbert's request for Noether to be employed as a junior professor, citing her gender. "I don't see why the sex of the candidate is relevant," Hilbert famously retorted. "This is after all an academic institution, not a bath house."[19] The institution refused to budge. Throughout her 18-year teaching career at Göttingen, Noether was never officially paid as a professor, though Hilbert scraped together a small stipend for her to lecture on algebra.

If Noether was disheartened by this, she never let it show. After all, she was doing some of the most important and revolutionary work of her life at Göttingen.

With her theorem, she uncovered the hidden relationship between symmetry and conservation, discovering that when an object or system in nature possesses symmetry – that is, the ability to look and behave as before even after undergoing change – there is also a corresponding law of conservation, such as the conservation of energy. Noether's theorem would go on to revolutionize science; it is now woven into our understanding of everything from the orbit of the planets to our search for the Higgs boson.

In 1933 Adolf Hitler was appointed Chancellor of Germany and ordered that all Jewish civil servants – including professors and teachers – had to be dismissed, unless they had served in the First World War. Noether, who once snickered when students turned up to lectures in Brownshirts, realized that Germany was quickly turning against the Jewish community. As a Jewish pacifist who had visited Moscow to meet Soviet mathematicians, she was right in the firing line.

Turned out of her own university, Noether fled the Nazis and gained employment at Bryn Mawr College in the US as a visiting professor. But she found brief respite on American shores and died less than two years after her arrival. In a letter to the *New York Times*, Einstein wrote of his dismay and sadness: "In the judgment of the most competent living mathematicians, Fräulein Noether was the most significant creative mathematical genius thus far produced since the higher education of women began."[20]

ofia Kovalevskaya (1850–1891) was introduced to numbers through a complete act of fate. As a child, she was far more enamoured with literature: "By the time I was twelve," she wrote in her memoirs, "I was unshakeably convinced that I was going to become a poet."[21] One day, her family accidentally ordered too little wallpaper for her childhood nursery and her father decided to paper over a bare wall with scrap paper from their attic, including his old lecture notes on differential and integral calculus.

Kovalevskaya was entranced by the wall. She would stand for hours in front of its mysterious symbols, trying to interpret their meaning. "Indeed, their very text left a deep trace in my brain, although they were incomprehensible to me while I was reading them."[22] Though her father abhorred "learned women" and shooed children away from the family library, Kovalevskaya was lucky enough to have an uncle who adored his bright and inquisitive niece. He mentioned mathematical concepts to her such as "squaring the circle…[and] many other things which were quite unintelligible to me and yet seemed mysterious and at the same time deeply attractive."[23]

When a neighbouring professor gave the family his textbook on elementary physics, Kovalevskaya threw herself into trying to understand it. But she was hindered by the dense trigonometric language, which she had never encountered before: what was a sine? Kovalevskaya eventually arrived at an answer herself through trial and error, which she explained to the astounded professor on his next visit. At 13, Kovalevskaya had independently figured out the meaning of a sine in exactly the same way that trained mathematicians had in the past.

Thanks to the professor's protestations at her wasted genius, Kovalevskaya's father reluctantly arranged for her to take private lessons in mathematics. But when it came to further education, 19th-century Russia did not welcome intelligent young women, including those who belonged to the landed gentry. Even travelling abroad was forbidden unless a woman was accompanied by a male chaperone.

Sofia was able to circumvent the ban with a bogus marriage to Vladimir Kovalevskaya, a women's rights advocate who believed that women should have access to education. Thanks to her fake nuptials, she was able to leave for Germany in 1869 to pursue mathematics. At the University of Heidelberg, Kovalevskaya's professors were enraptured by her brilliance. As one classmate remembered, "talk of the amazing Russian woman spread through the little town, so that people would often stop in the street to stare at her."[24]

European universities, however, were still as stuck in the past as Russian society. Kovalevskaya could go to lectures at Heidelberg only in an unofficial capacity; the University of Berlin, where she was desperate to study under the great Karl Weierstrass, didn't allow women to enter the lecture hall at all. Fortunately, Weierstrass was so impressed with Kovalevskaya's ability that he agreed to take her on as a private student. Under his tutelage, she produced three doctoral dissertations and, with some arm-twisting on Weierstrass's part, she was able to present them at the University of Göttingen, which had awarded degrees to women and foreigners in the past. In the summer of 1874, Kovalevskaya became the first woman in Europe with a Ph.D in mathematics based solely on the strength of her three pieces of work, all without attending a single class at Göttingen.

For the next six years, however, Kovalevskaya's intelligence would be rerouted into family life as her marriage of convenience blossomed into a real romance. But she was never cut out for "the soft slime of bourgeois existence,"[25] as she put it. Her marriage to Kovalevsky collapsed and she finally gained a teaching position at a more welcoming university in 1883. Even so, as an assistant professor at the University of Stockholm, she drew no staff salary except for private fees paid by students. Six months after her first lecture, however, the university was impressed enough to appoint her as a full professor of mathematics.

Her talent finally recognized, Kovalevskaya plunged into intellectual life and promptly pursued one of mathematics' greatest challenges. The French Academy of Sciences offered 3,000 francs to anyone who could make a significant contribution toward explaining the "rotation of a solid body around a fixed point",[26] a problem in mechanical physics that had dogged academics for so long that it was known as "the mathematical mermaid".[27] With great fanfare, Kovalevskaya's work was selected out of 15 anonymous entries as the winner. It was judged so outstanding that her cash prize was increased to 5,000 francs.

In a move that would have delighted her 12-year-old self, Kovalevskaya also began to dabble in writing, including a play, journalistic articles, an acclaimed fiction book and even her own childhood memoirs. "You are surprised at my working simultaneously in literature and in mathematics," she wrote in a letter to a friend. "It seems to me that the poet must see what others do not see, must see more deeply than other people. And the mathematician must do the same."[28]

Kovalevskaya had finally found a way to reconcile her childhood dream of letters with her adult passion of numbers. But in 1891, she caught pneumonia – a death sentence in a world before antibiotics. She died six days after her diagnosis. If she hadn't passed away at the age of 41, who knows how she would have gone on to reshape her discipline? As she put it herself: "Mathematics has always seemed to me a science which opens up completely new horizons."[29]

ophie Germain (1776–1831) was only 13 when the French Revolution quite literally began in her Parisian neighbourhood. Violent riots against Louis XVI engulfed the streets seconds away from her family home on rue Saint-Denis, and she lived only 500 metres (550 yards) away from La Conciergerie, where Marie Antoinette was locked up shortly before her execution in 1793, when Germain was 17 years old.

Germain's parents were relatively well off and did their best to protect their children from the anarchy happening beyond the walls of their house. As the Reign of Terror raged outside, Germain retreated to the family library, where she read a book on the history of mathematics that laid out the grisly killing of Archimedes at the Siege of Syracuse. She was spellbound by the story of the Greek mathematician so wrapped up in a geometry problem that he failed to notice the murderous Roman soldier in his room; it made her determined to study the discipline for which Archimedes had sacrificed his life.

Much to the consternation of her family, she began studying every book on mathematics in the library. This was behaviour most unbecoming of both her age and gender. Her parents tried to discourage it by removing her warm clothes and all sources of heat and light from her bedroom, reasoning that this would stop her from staying up and reading through the night.

But they had underestimated just how starved their daughter was of intellectual stimulation. Once everyone in the house had gone to bed, Germain would wrap bedsheets around herself and begin her studies by candlelight. In the mornings, she was found fast sleep over a desk of calculations, her ink frozen in its well. Her parents eventually yielded and allowed her to do as she wished.

This victory wasn't as straightforward as it seemed. To lay her hands on actual academic material, Germain had to become a master of subterfuge. Though women were not admitted to the newly established École Polytechnique in Paris, she managed to obtain the lecture notes and began corresponding with a professor named Joseph-Louis Lagrange under the pretence that she was a male student named Monsieur Le Blanc. At some point, however, the ruse was discovered and Germain became an academic sensation; scholars including Lagrange attempted to assist in her learning, passing her papers and notes. Crucially, however, none of them were able to get her into any schools of higher learning where she might receive what she sought most: a professional scientific education.

Instead, Germain contented herself with writing letters to various experts and intellectuals, including the German mathematician Carl Friedrich Gauss. Fearing "the ridicule associated with being a female scholar",[30] she again resorted to her old pen name of Le Blanc and struck up a correspondence with Gauss, who was widely believed to be the greatest mathematician since antiquity. In her letters she made bold inroads in proving Fermat's Last Theorem and unknowingly became the first woman to attempt to tackle the famously sticky proof.

$$N^2 \left(\frac{\partial^4 z}{\partial x^4} + \frac{\partial^4 z}{\partial x^2 \partial y^2} + \frac{\partial^4 z}{\partial y^4} \right) + \frac{\partial^2 z}{\partial t^2} = 0$$

"Unfortunately," she wrote to Gauss, "the depth of my intellect does not equal the voracity of my appetite, and I feel a kind of temerity in troubling a man of genius when I have no other claim to his attention than an admiration necessarily shared by all his readers."[31]

Gauss was delighted by the letters and began swapping work with his young admirer, encouraging and offering critical feedback to "Monsieur Le Blanc". When Germain's true identity was rumbled, her older mentor was astonished: "The scientific notes with which your letters are so richly filled have given me a thousand pleasures. I have studied them with attention, and I admire the ease with which you penetrate all branches of arithmetic, and the wisdom with which you generalize and perfect."[32]

When Germain was 33, Napoléon Bonaparte became fascinated by a discovery made by physicist Ernst Chladni, who found that sand on a glass plate would vibrate and collect in strange geometric formations when a bow was rubbed against the glass. He ordered that the French Academy of Sciences should award a one-kilogram (approximately one-and-a-quarter-pound) gold medal to anyone who could explain the mysterious phenomena.

Never one to back down from a challenge, Germain became the competition's first and only entrant, but her equation was off. When the competition was extended, she made a second attempt – again as the only entrant – and received an honourable mention. A third go won her the prize and the admiration of her scientific colleagues.

She was finally allowed into lectures at the École Polytechnique and became the first unmarried woman to attend sessions at the Academy of Sciences. Her work on the vibration of surfaces is used today in to build skyscrapers and in the field of acoustics. In the words of her mentor Gauss: "A woman because of her sex and our prejudices encounters infinitely more obstacles than a man in familiarizing herself with complicated problems. Yet when she overcomes these barriers and penetrates that which is most hidden, she undoubtedly possesses the most noble courage, extraordinary talent and superior genius."[33]

$$N^2 \left(\frac{\partial^4 z}{\partial x^4} + \frac{\partial^4 z}{\partial x^2 \partial y^2} + \frac{\partial^4 z}{\partial y^4} \right) + \frac{\partial^2 z}{\partial t^2} =$$

Technology & Inventions

ny good scientist knows that you're only as good as your tools, but few people are aware that some of the world's earliest lab apparatus was invented in the 2nd or 3rd century AD by a woman. In her day, **Maria the Jewess** (c.AD 2nd–3rd century), also known as Maria the Prophetess or Maria Prophetissa), was revered as one of the great alchemists of the ancient world.

She is believed to have published major works of alchemy – making her history's first female Jewish author – including one called *Maria Practica*, though little remains of her writing and research. What we do know of her comes from second-hand accounts of admiring followers such as Zosimus of Panopolis, the 4th-century Egyptian alchemist who quoted her work extensively in his writings and nicknamed her "the Divine Maria".

Before chemistry became better associated with white lab coats and precision-engineered equipment, it existed in the murky world of alchemy. Here, the study of elements had as much to do with magic and spirituality as it did with science. As Maria noted: "Just as man is composed of four elements, likewise is copper; and just as a man results [from the association of] liquids, of solids, and of the spirit, so does copper."[1] Alchemists like Maria saw God in the transmutation of chemicals; in their search for the Philosopher's Stone – the mysterious substance able to transform base metals into gold – a quest for divinity. Maria is said to have been one of four women capable of conjuring the legendary Stone, which was also rumoured to bestow immortality. According to Zosimus, she was the first alchemist to prepare copper and sulphur to create the raw material required for gold.

Maria saw religion as instrumental to her journey to discover what alchemists referred to as the "Great Work".

Jews, after all, were seen as God's chosen people and Maria believed that only they could hope to understand the innermost secrets of alchemy. She warned gentile alchemists not to touch the Philosopher's Stone with their bare hands: "If you are not of our race, you cannot touch it, for the Art is special, not common."[2] She must have guarded its mysteries closely, for the obsession to discover the Philosopher's Stone consumed alchemists up until the 17th century.

But Maria's work does live on in scientific instruments that people continue to use today: if you've ever used a double boiler in the kitchen, you can already count yourself familiar with one of her greatest inventions. In fact, the alternative name for a double boiler should provide a clue: the bain-marie, which derives its name from the Latin *balneum Mariae*, or "Mary's bath". Maria is thought to have devised this water bath, which allows a substance in an inner vessel to be slowly and evenly heated by steam arising from water boiling in an outer vessel.

Along with the Babylonian female chemist Tapputi (see page 140), Maria was one of the first people to describe the use of a still: a three-pronged apparatus that enables the distillation of substances by means of evaporation and condensation. She was constantly seeking to improve her lab equipment, concocting ovens and stills from various materials, refining and caulking them with everything from clay to wax. Her *tribikos* – an alchemical still with three separate copper spouts – allowed vaporized chemicals to condense and drip down these ports and on to plates of different metals, so that Maria could note their reaction to the original chemical. The observations she made about the equipment still hold up today. She explained her preference for glass vessels because they "see without touching" and allowed her to handle substances without contamination, as well as otherwise dangerous ingredients such as mercury.

Maria's work was cited by alchemists into the Middle Ages. After her death, the legends around her grew so convoluted and epic that at one point there were various competing reports that she was Moses' sister Miriam; that she had received a vision of Christ on a mountain; that she was the daughter of an Arabic king; and that she carried the baby Jesus on her own shoulder. In recent times, she languished in obscurity until she was rediscovered by the cultural anthropologist and Jewish scholar Raphael Patai, who said that she "deserves to be styled the founding mother of Western alchemy".[3]

Today, the quest for the Philosopher's Stone has long passed into the realm of apocryphal myth and children's fantasy, but Maria's great inventions are still used in households around the world every day. The next time you reach for the double boiler in your kitchen, remember that you're using a piece of equipment made by a woman whose fantastical exploits were nearly lost to the world.

MARY BEATRICE DAVIDSON KENNER

ary Beatrice Davidson Kenner (1912–2006) always had trouble sleeping when she was growing up in Charlotte, North Carolina. Her mother would leave for work in the morning through the squeaky door at the back of their house and the noise would wake Kenner up. "So I said one day, 'Mom, don't you think someone could invent a self-oiling door hinge?'"[4] She was only six at the time, but she set about the task with all the seriousness of a born inventor. "I [hurt] my hands trying to make something that, in my mind, would be good for the door," she said. "After that I dropped it, but never forgot it."[5]

You could say that skill and ingenuity was in Kenner's blood. Her maternal grandfather had invented a tricolour light signal to guide trains, and her sister, Mildred Davidson Austin Smith, grew up to patent her own family board game and sell it commercially. Her preacher father, Sidney Nathaniel Davidson, even made a go of transforming the family hobby into a full-time career. Around 1914, Sidney patented a clothes presser that would fit in a suitcase and press trousers while a traveller was en route to his destination, but he turned down a New York company's $20,000 offer in favour of attempting to manufacture and sell it himself. The result was a failure: he produced only a single presser, which he sold for the paltry sum of $14.

Her father's experience didn't put Kenner off inventing, and her idea for the door hinge ignited a spark deep inside her. New ideas for inventions would wake her up from sleep. She occupied herself drawing up models and building them.. While other children her age were drawing fanciful aeroplanes and sports cars,

180

May 15, 1956   B. KENNER   2,745,406
                           SANITARY BELT
                         Filed July 20, 1954

Fig.1

10

12

14

Fig.3

18   16

20

Fig.2

16

24   26

22

18   20

26

32   Fig.4

28   30

30

24

26

4

30

28

4

Beatrice Kenner
INVENTOR

BY

Kenner was making thoughtful plans for a convertible roof that would go over the folding rumble seat of a car, where back-seat passengers were usually exposed to the elements. When she saw water dripping off a closed umbrella and onto the floor, she came up with a sponge tip that would go on the end and soak up the rainwater. She even drew up plans for a portable ashtray that would attach itself to a cigarette packet.

This pragmatic, do-it-yourself approach defined her inventions for the rest of her life. But while her creations were often geared toward sensible solutions for everyday problems, Kenner could tell from an early age that she had a skill that not many possessed. When her family moved to Washington DC in 1924, Kenner would stalk the halls of the United States Patent and Trademark Office, trying to work out if someone had beaten her to it and filed a patent for an invention first. The 12-year-old didn't find any that had done so.

In 1931 Kenner graduated from high school and earned a place at the prestigious Howard University, but was forced to drop out a year and a half into her course due to financial pressures. She took on odd jobs such as babysitting before landing a position as a federal employee, but she continued tinkering in her spare time. The perennial problem was money; filing a patent was, and is, an expensive business. Today, a basic utility patent can cost several hundred dollars.

By 1957 Kenner had saved enough money to file her first ever patent: a belt for sanitary napkins. It was long before the advent of disposable pads, and women were still using cloth pads and rags during their period. Kenner proposed an adjustable belt with an inbuilt, moisture-proof napkin pocket, making it less likely that menstrual blood could leak and stain clothes.

"One day I was contacted by a company that expressed an interest in marketing my idea. I was so jubilant," she said. "I saw houses, cars, and everything about to come my way." A company rep drove to Kenner's house in Washington to meet with their prospective client. "Sorry to say, when they found out I was black, their interest dropped. The representative went back to New York and informed me the company was no longer interested."[6]

Undeterred, Kenner continued inventing for all her adult life. She eventually filed five patents in total, more than any other African-American woman in history. Again, she continued to draw inspiration from her daily life. When her sister Mildred developed multiple sclerosis and had to get around with a walking frame, Kenner patented a serving tray and a soft pocket that could be attached to the frame, allowing Mildred to carry things around with her. She also patented a toilet tissue holder that made sure that the loose end of a roll was always within reach, and a back washer that could be attached to the wall of a shower to help people clean hard-to-reach parts of their back.

Kenner did not receive any college degree or professional training, and she never became rich from her inventions. But that was incidental; like her father and grandfather before her, she did it out of love for the craft. Most of all, she believed that anyone could become an inventor as long as they put their mind to it: "Every person is born with a creative mind," she said. "Everyone has that ability."[7]

n 1890, a London housewife named **Hertha Ayrton** (1854–1923) was struggling to balance the demands of domesticity, her newborn daughter and her true love: science. As the daughter of a Jewish watchmaker from Poland, Ayrton had spent time tinkering with various devices while studying for her mathematics degree at Cambridge; she had invented a line-divider that could split a line into equal sections and even constructed a sphygmograph for recording one's pulse. Her brilliant mind won her a nickname from her family: B.G., or Beautiful Genius. But now she had little free time to focus on her studies and it seemed like she would have to give up altogether.

Then Madame Barbara Bodichon stepped in. As the co-founder of the first women's college at Cambridge, Madame Bodichon was the one who had interviewed Ayrton during her application and arranged a loan for the promising student to attend university. When Ayrton wanted to take out a patent on her line-divider, it was Madame Bodichon who provided the cash for it. Even after her death, she was looking out for Ayrton: when Madame Bodichon died in 1891, she bequeathed enough money to her friend and protégée to hire a housekeeper, freeing her up to pursue research.

Ayrton had a knack for divining the truth from everyday mysteries and then extrapolating an invention from there. A holiday to the English seaside town of Margate inspired her to examine the link between the water's waves and the corresponding ripples in sandbanks. When Ayrton heard that chlorine and mustard gas were slaughtering British soldiers fighting in the First World War, she applied her theory about water ripples to a device that could use the movement of air to push away the deadly airborne weapon. The resulting device, the Ayrton fan, was mass-produced and shipped in vast quantities to the Western Front, saving countless lives.

One of her greatest discoveries quite literally illuminated London. In the late 1800s arc lighting had replaced gas and oil in street lamps as the first commercially viable form of electric light. But the technology wasn't perfect: the lamps constantly hissed and flickered. Ayrton's husband William – an electrical engineer by training and a professor at Finsbury Technical College – was trying to work out a way to make a more reliable arc light. Unfortunately, his research was destroyed when a maid accidentally used the notes as kindling for a fire. When William was too busy to start again, Ayrton decided to tackle the challenge alone.

As she duplicated William's experiments, she realized that the annoying hiss could be traced to the oxidation of carbon rods used in an arc lamp. By redesigning the rods and making sure that they didn't come into direct contact with the oxygen, she could dramatically reduce the noise and flickering. Between 1895 and 1896, she published 12 articles in *The Electrician*. In the same year, she was the first woman to present a paper to the Institution of Electrical Engineers and was immediately elected a member as a result.

It would be a longer and more torturous road to wider recognition, beginning with the Royal Society. At its headquarters in Burlington House, the top scientists gathered to discuss its fellows' research. Women, however, had never been admitted past its doors. In fact, when Ayrton's paper, *The Mechanism of the Electric Arc*, was to be presented to the Society in 1901, its members enlisted a man to read it out. When she was proposed as a fellow, the Royal Society decided to exclude her: "We are of the opinion that married women are not eligible as Fellows of the Royal Society...Whether the Charters admit of the election of unmarried women appears to us to be very doubtful."[8]

"Personally I do not agree with sex being brought into science at all," she told a journalist at the time. "The idea of 'women and science' is entirely irrelevant. Either a woman is a good scientist or she is not; in any case she should be given opportunities, and her work should be studied from the scientific, not the sex, point of view."[9] She was still denied Royal Society membership, even after the Society awarded her the Hughes Medal for her work on electricity.

It was little wonder that Ayrton took up the suffragette cause around this time. She joined the Women's Social and Political Union in 1906 and was attacked by a police officer while marching to Downing Street with Emmeline Pankhurst. When her daughter Barbara was arrested, she gushed in a letter, "Barbie is in Holloway...I am *very* proud of her."[10] When Pankhurst and other hunger strikers left prison, starved and frail, Ayrton helped to nurse them back to recovery.

Ayrton never forgot her first woman mentor, the one who had done so much to advance her career. When her book *The Electric Arc* was published in 1902, she dedicated it to Madame Bodichon, "whose clearsighted enthusiasm for the freedom and enlightenment of women enabled her to strike away so many barriers from their path...to her whose friendship changed and beautified my whole life".[11]

n the autumn of 1947, **Admiral Grace Hopper** (1906–1992) found a bug in her computer. It was a literal insect; a moth, to be precise. The United States Navy lieutenant retrieved its body from the bowels of the malfunctioning Harvard Mark I machine and taped it firmly into her logbook, noting wryly: "First actual case of bug being found."[12]

Throughout her trailblazing career as a pioneer of computer coding, Hopper retained her droll sense of humour. When asked if there was a celebration party when she left the Navy at the age of 80, the decorated US rear admiral replied: "I was asleep. It's something you learn in your first boot camp: if they put you down somewhere with nothing to do, go to sleep."[13]

Hopper was 37 when she enlisted in the Navy, spurred on by the idea of helping her country during the Second World War. She left behind a promising career as a college professor to report for duty at a Navy officer school and was initially deemed too advanced in age and too petite to serve in the military. Fortunately, she was also in the unique position of being one of the only women in the US with a mathematics doctorate. Hopper assumed that would make her a natural fit in a code-breaking unit, but her commanding officers had bigger plans for her: she was sent to a basement in Harvard to work on a gargantuan IBM machine called the Automatic Sequence Controlled Calculator, or Mark I for short. Hopper didn't realize it at the time, but she was to become one of three programmers of the world's first computer.

The Mark I was 15 metres (51 feet) long, weighed almost 4550 kilograms (10,000 pounds) and was theoretically capable of performing the kind of complex calculations the Navy needed in order to work out tricky problems such as rocket trajectories, wind speeds and ship infrastructure. In short, all the difficult sums that were necessary to win a war. But the Mark I was a temperamental beast: anything could throw off its calculations, including frayed machine parts or aforementioned insects, and Hopper often went hunting along the length of the machine for hardware bugs with a small mirror. She grew to recognize every whirr, creak and sigh of the Mark I as if it were her own child. By the time the war ended, Hopper was asked to write the first operation manual for the Mark I, as well as for its successor, the Mark II.

When Hopper left the Navy, she worked for Remington Rand, a private company that had started out in the typewriter business. As the senior programmer, she grew convinced that the programming language needed to be simplified so that it was quicker to write and easier to learn. Computers could already store bits of code that could be conveniently re-used: why not assign these so-called subroutines specific call numbers so that they could be deployed more efficiently? Come to think of it, why not just allocate them words in English?

"No-one thought of that earlier, because they weren't as lazy as I was," Hopper claimed modestly.[14] She developed the first compiler in her spare time: a library of automated computing language that was constantly expanding, thanks to a community of mathematicians and programmers who would develop and contribute bits of new code.

Hopper's user-generated compiler led to the development of COBOL (Common Business Oriented Language), the first programming language for business. And, just as Hopper wished, you didn't need to have a mathematics doctorate to understand it: most of it was written in English.

Over Hopper's lifetime, she saw computers shrink from huge machines to desktop PCs. In 1992, the year of her death, another revolution in computing was taking place in the form of the first smartphone: IBM's Simon Personal Communicator. Today, smart home devices such as Alexa and Google Home promise hands-free computing. Hopper, who always wanted to make computing usable by everyone, would have been delighted by the leap in technology. By the time she passed away, she had gained recognition as an early pioneer of the computer revolution and had been awarded eight medals for her service to the US. In 2016, the Presidential Medal of Freedom was added to her list posthumously.

As for Hopper's bug, it found a distinguished resting place appropriate for its role in computing science; it now sits in the Smithsonian's National Museum of American History in Washington DC.

ong before the word "computer" came to denote a desktop PC or Mac, it was used to refer to people – in fact, mostly women – who could perform the kind of complicated mathematical calculations that would leave the brainiest number-puzzle enthusiast scratching their head.

With the advent of the Second World War and the military call-up, companies and businesses across the US began opening their doors to women and ethnic minorities who had been otherwise excluded from industry. The Langley Research Center at NASA (National Aeronautics and Space Administration), then known as the National Advisory Committee for Aeronautics (NACA), was no different; by 1946, Langley had employed 400 women computers, many of them science graduates attracted to the relatively high pay and the promise of working in aeronautics at America's premier space agency.

At the time, women found it almost impossible to secure a job as a scientist or engineer, and many a smart and ambitious college leaver had to settle for a job teaching high school science instead. And if you were a black woman? Well, you could pretty much forget it, which makes the story of **The West Computers** even more remarkable.

When necessity prompted Langley to start adding women of colour to its computing pool, segregation was still standard office policy. Despite doing exactly the same work as their white counterparts, the West Computers were cloistered in the West Area of Langley (hence their nickname) and had separate bathrooms and cafeteria tables. One computer, Miriam Mann of Covington, Georgia, was so incensed by the sign denoting where the "coloured girls" should sit while dining that she repeatedly removed it. "She brought the first one home, but there was a replacement the next day," her daughter, Miriam Mann Harris, remembered.[15]

Mann wasn't the only West Computer who engaged in small but vital acts of rebellion. When Katherine Johnson – a West Virginia State College maths graduate, who was so exceptional that her professor was compelled to put on advanced courses just for her – was appointed as computer to the Flight Research Division, she simply refused to use the segregated facilities. Instead, she used the unmarked bathroom and ate her lunch at her desk, just like her white colleagues.

If a missile or aeroplane ever took off successfully, you could bet that the pencils of the West Computers had worked out the sums that kept it in the air. Though the calculations that the West Computers performed were bafflingly complex and sophisticated, the women were categorized as sub-professional aides and almost always regarded as anonymous tools. The real stars of the show – the aerospace engineers – would pass on huge chunks of data and expect the women to churn out analysis, often without even explaining how the research was being used.

But as the work grew increasingly complicated, an outstanding computer could catch the attention of engineers working on specific projects. Former bookkeeper and clerk typist Mary Jackson was one of these women. Two years after she was initially employed, she was assigned to the Langley wind tunnels dedicated to cracking supersonic and hypersonic flight, and was deemed impressive enough to attend Langley's engineer training programme. She had to petition local government to allow her to attend the required classes at the all-white Hampton High School, and after graduating she became one of the first female engineers at NACA.

By the mid-1950s, the ranks of the West Computers had shrunk as members found new opportunities in Langley's engineering labs. The agency had already shut down the East Computing pool in 1947, and West Computing followed suit in 1958 as NACA was transformed into NASA.

If Dorothy "Dot" Vaughan was saddened by the closure of her department, she didn't let it show. The former head of the West Computers had joined in 1943 and was the first black supervisor at the agency, fighting all the way for the equal pay and rights of the women under her.

Vaughan transformed herself into one of NASA's leading computer programmers, overseeing the IBM machines that would soon replace human computers altogether. (In the beginning, even astronaut John Glenn didn't trust the newfangled contraptions. Before he became the first American to orbit earth, he famously weighed up the mathematical prowess of Johnson against an electronic computer and said: "Get the girl to check the numbers."[16])

As the decades wore on, the former West Computers distinguished themselves as researchers and engineers as well as advocates for women in science. Johnson's brainpower helped to send Glenn into space, but she carved out time to visit students and inspire them with her story. At the age of 58, Jackson chose to give up her job as an engineer to become the Federal Women's Programme Manager at NASA, to make it easier for other women and minorities to make it in her field.

Johnson is one of the few West Computers still alive and, at the age of 99, she was catapulted to international fame with the biography and Oscar-winning biopic *Hidden Figures* (2016), which dramatized the heady decades of the space race. "There's nothing to it – I was just doing my job," she shrugged when the *Washington Post* came knocking. "They needed information and I had it, and it didn't matter that I found it. At the time, it was just a question and an answer."[17]

f you log on to the internet on your smartphone or desktop every day, it's easy to forget that you're accessing the world's biggest repository of information: bigger than the Library of Alexandria, more in-depth than any collection of encyclopedias and more knowledgable than any human on the planet. Imagine a massive network of millions of computers humming with activity, communicating with each other from countries all over the world. Who helped to make that happen? **Rose Dieng-Kuntz** (1956–2008), that's who.

Dieng-Kuntz grew up in Dakar, the busy capital of Senegal, as one of seven siblings. Her father was born to an illiterate and impoverished single mother; school was the only way out for him and he passed on that lesson to all his children. It was something that Dieng-Kuntz never forgot (she ended up dedicating her Irène Joliot-Curie Prize to him in 2005). When a primary school teacher admonished her in class saying, "You Africans are less clever than the whites. You should make sure you pay attention!",[18] Dieng-Kuntz didn't just sit up and pay closer attention. She came top in her high school class in mathematics, French and Latin, and won a scholarship to the prestigious École Polytechnique in Paris (the same institution that had denied women including French mathematician Sophie Germain a place almost two hundred years earlier, see page 172). In the process, she became the first African woman to walk through its halls as a student.

Dieng-Kuntz had originally dreamed of becoming a writer, but her teachers nudged her in the direction of mathematics. She graduated with a doctorate degree in information technology and joined the French Institute for Research in Computer Science and Automation (INRIA) as a computer scientist. In 1985 she began conducting research into artificial intelligence (AI). At the time, AI research was dominated by a type of program known as an expert system, which relied on a set knowledge base to make the same kind of decisions and logical inferences as a human expert. Dieng-Kuntz was one of the leaders in the field when it came to making expert systems as efficient and effective as possible.

"A woman, a black woman, and a specialist in artificial intelligence: I found myself smack bang in the middle of a lot of minority groups," Dieng-Kuntz once told *Le Monde* newspaper. "They thought I was some kind of masochist…But I haven't suffered in my work."[19]

When the world wide web was invented in 1989, Dieng-Kuntz quickly grasped its revolutionary potential. After all, she was interested in the communication – how information is acquired, classified and shared – and how best to nurture the networks that foster the vital broadening of knowledge. Her work had life-changing implications for society. At the INRIA Sophia Antipolis – Méditerranée research centre in Nice, she headed up the multidisciplinary Acacia project and worked to create healthcare software that gave doctors and medical staff a virtual way to share information about cases, allowing them to build a better understanding of a patient's needs and determine the best possible treatments. Dieng-Kuntz's research on knowledge modelling and acquisition – which she laid out in dozens of scientific articles and books – now forms part of the backbone of the web.

Despite settling in France, the internet pioneer never lost sight of her roots or her own journey from Senegal, a former French colony. "It's a history based on a lot of suffering," she said. "My generation, which didn't know colonialism first hand, should always have it in our minds... I believe in the strength of symbols," she added. To Dieng-Kuntz, speaking out and being visible were vital to "demonstrate that a black woman can blossom in the world of scientific research, in France, and take on responsibilities, and transfer this passion on to young people, particularly to young girls."[20]

When she passed away in 2008, INRIA Sophia Antipolis – Méditerranée's director, Michel Cosnard, hailed Dieng-Kuntz's visionary spirit: "Just after the invention of the web and well before its widespread use around the world, what insight [she had] to envisage its applications, understand its limits and decipher its evolution."[21] But in the 21st century, there's no better tribute to Dieng-Kuntz than to see her dream of "a web of knowledge linking individuals, organisations, countries and continents"[22] more alive than ever.

y 1843, **Ada Lovelace** (1815–1852) had hypothesized that a machine could be more than just a number-crunching object: it could compose elaborate music, predict lunar cycles and perform all kinds of complicated mathematical and scientific tasks. In short, it could do everything that computers can do now. Today, the Victorian founder of modern computing is celebrated as the world's first computer programmer, but it took more than a century for her visionary ideas to be recognized.

In 1815 Lovelace was born to the Romantic poet Lord Byron and his wife, Annabella Byron. Both parents were wildly intelligent polar opposites: Byron, as former lover Lady Caroline Lamb described him, the "mad, bad, and dangerous to know" writer[23], and Annabella the strict and morally upright baroness. When Byron abandoned both Ada and Annabella two months after Ada's birth, Annabella grew deeply concerned that their daughter would inherit Byron's worst excesses, both emotionally and morally. (Given that Byron's first words to his child were "what an implement of torture have I acquired in you", this was perhaps understandable.[24]) To this end, she shied away from cultivating Ada's creative imagination and instead nurtured her skill in mathematics. It was clear that Lovelace had the unique ability to synthesize the two from an early age; at 12, she dreamed up a winged, steam-powered flying machine inspired by her study of birds, illustrated with careful reference to potentially airborne materials such as feathers and silk. One of her tutors, the English mathematician Augustus De Morgan, even warned her mother that Lovelace's capacity for scientific thinking could affect her health: "The very great tension of mind which [mathematics] require is beyond the strength of a woman's physical power of application."[25]

Just before she turned 18, Lovelace made her society debut at the royal court and met a 44-year-old mathematician named Charles Babbage, a co-founder of the Royal Astronomical Society. Babbage had created a prototype for a hand-cranked contraption he called the Difference Engine, which was intended to calculate mathematical tables automatically.

Lovelace was enthralled when she saw the device in Babbage's drawing room at Dorset Street, London, though it was far from a working specimen. This chance encounter launched a long and fruitful friendship and a lengthy correspondence between the two great minds. Babbage was deeply impressed by Lovelace's intellect, gushing to the inventor Michael Faraday that she was an "Enchantress who has thrown her magical spell around the most abstract of Sciences and has grasped it with a force which few masculine intellects (in our own country at least) could have exerted over it."[26]

In 1834 Babbage began working on something he called the Analytical Engine, which he envisaged as a great improvement on the Difference Engine in terms of accuracy. He sketched out ideas for a huge device containing 20,000 cogwheels and operated by a punch-card system, like the Jacquard weaving looms that had come into fashion in Victorian England.

Family obligations briefly interrupted Lovelace's correspondence with Babbage – she married in 1835 and gave birth to three children soon after – but she never lost her taste for mathematics. By this time, her old friend's machine had run into difficulties; for one thing, it was far too expensive for Babbage to build by himself. He hoped that by giving lectures to publicize his proposal, he might entice the government or a wealthy donor to invest. When an Italian scientist wrote a paper about the engine based on one such lecture, Lovelace went above and beyond the call of friendship in translating it: she penned a 20,000-word series of notes intended to enhance the understanding of the paper, which ended up laying the foundations for modern computing.

Babbage had envisaged the engine as nothing more than a highly accurate device to carry out mathematical calculations, but Lovelace glimpsed something deeper and more profound in its whirring cogs and gear shafts. She saw the future: "The science of operations, as derived from mathematics more especially," she wrote, "is a science of itself, and has its own abstract truth and value." This "science of operations," as historian James Essinger notes[27], is no less than the science of computing itself.

If a Jacquard loom could translate and create complex patterns from punch cards in silk, the same could be done with Babbage's machine. Any information – numbers, musical notation and the like – could be digitized, translated and processed into such patterns. One section of Lovelace's *Notes* even lays out the step-by-step "operations" necessary for the punch cards to automate a long sequence of Bernoulli numbers, a type of sequence of rational numbers, now thought to be the first example of a computer program.

While Babbage had invented the Engine, it was Lovelace who saw its potential to create a whole field of science in itself. She hadn't even meant to take credit for it, either: it was her husband who had to prompt her to sign her lengthy treatise. She dutifully inserted the initials AAL: Augusta Ada Lovelace.

The Difference Engine was never built, and Lovelace became fatally ill in 1852 and died that winter. Her *Notes* languished in obscurity before it was republished as part of English scientist B V Bowden's 1953 book *Faster Than Thought: A Symposium on Digital Computing Machines*. The advent of "electronic brains,"[28] as Bowden puts it, had more in common with Lovelace's genius foresight than with Babbage's Engine. As for the "vast… and a powerful language" that she predicted[29], a variation of it now bears her name in the form of a programming language called Ada. Today, it powers underground trains, Boeing 777s, satellites and rockets: a fitting tribute for someone whose first scientific forays were inspired by flight.

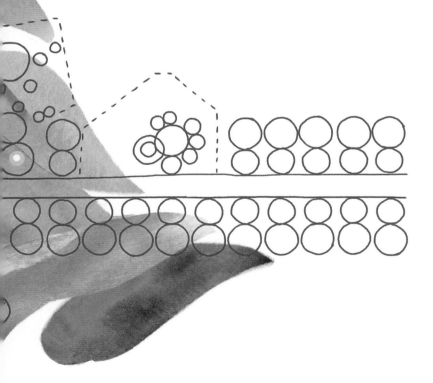

Introduction

1 Chambers, David Wade. "Stereotypic images of the scientist: The Draw-a-Scientist Test". *Science Education* 67.2, 1983: 255–65.

2 www.wisecampaign.org.uk/resources/2016/11/women-in-the-stem-workforce-2016. Accessed 17 September, 2017

3 www.esa.doc.gov/reports/women-stem-gender-gap-innovation. Accessed 17 September, 2017

4 www.varsity.co.uk/news/6433. Accessed 17 September, 2017

5 Payne-Gaposchkin, Cecilia. *Cecilia Payne-Gaposchkin: an autobiography and other recollections.* Cambridge University Press, 1996: 219

THE EARTH & THE UNIVERSE

1. Sobel, Dava. *The Glass Universe: The Hidden History of the Women Who Took the Measure of the Stars,* HarperCollins Publishers.
2. Lehmann, Inge. "Seismology in the days of old". *Eos, Transactions American Geophysical Union* 68.3, 1987: 35.
3. Bolt, Bruce A. "Inge Lehmann. 13 May 1888 – 21 February 1993". 1997: 287–301.
4. www.amnh.org/explore/resource-collections/earth-inside-and-out/inge-lehmann-discoverer-of-the-earth-s-inner-core/. Accessed 31 August, 2017
5. Lehmann, Inge. "Seismology in the days of old". *Eos, Transactions American Geophysical Union* 68.3, 1987: 33–5.

6. Bolt, Bruce A. "Inge Lehmann. 13 May 1888–21 February 1993". 1997: 287–301.
7. Haramundanis, Katherine (ed.). Cecilia Payne-Gaposchkin: *An Autobiography and Other Recollections,* Cambridge University Press, 1996: 86.
8. Ibid.: 227
9. Ibid.: 220.
10. Ibid.: 219.
11. Ibid.: 221.
12. Ibid.: 163.
13. Ibid.: 165.
14. Struve, Otto, and Zebergs, Velta. *Astronomy of the 20th Century,* Macmillan, 1962: 220.
15. Haramundanis, Katherine (ed.). Cecilia Payne-Gaposchkin: *An Autobiography and Other Recollections,* Cambridge University Press, 1996: 221.
16. Ibid.: 190.
17. Ibid.: 197.
18. Ibid.: 227.
19. Peterson, Barbara Bennett. *Notable Women of China: Shang Dynasty to the Early Twentieth Century,* Routledge, 2016.
20. Ko, Dorothy. "Pursuing talent and virtue: education and women's culture in seventeenth- and eighteenth-century China". *Late Imperial China* 13.1, 1992: 9–39.
21. Bernardi, Gabriella. *The Unforgotten Sisters: Female Astronomers and Scientists Before Caroline Herschel,* Springer, 2016: 158.
22. Ibid.: 156.
23. Peterson, Barbara Bennett. *Notable Women of China: Shang Dynasty to the Early Twentieth Century,* Routledge, 2016.
24. Bernardi, Gabriella. *The Unforgotten Sisters: Female Astronomers and Scientists Before Caroline Herschel,* Springer, 2016: 158.
25. Bruck, Mary T. "Alice Everett and Annie Russell Maunder torch bearing women astronomers". *Irish Astronomical Journal* 21, 1994: 281.
26. Ibid.
27. Ibid.
28. Evershed, M A. "Obituary notices:– Maunder, Annie Scott Dill". *Monthly Notices of the Royal Astronomical Society* 108: 48.
29. Maunder, Annie S D and E Walter. *The Heavens and Their Story,* R Culley, 1908: 7
30. Maunder, Annie S.D. and E. Walter. *The Heavens and Their Story.* R. Culley, 1908: 346

31. www.naa.gov.au/collection/snapshots/find-of-the-month/2009-march.aspx Accessed 22 August, 2017
32. Ibid.
33. www.abc.net.au/radionational/programs/scienceshow/ruby-payne-scott---radio-astronomer/3403336#transcript Accessed 22 August, 2017

BIOLOGY & NATURAL SCIENCES

1. Torrens, Hugh. "Presidential address: Mary Anning (1799–1847) of Lyme; 'the greatest fossilist the world ever knew'". *The British Journal for the History of Science* 28.3, 1995: 269, www.jstor.org/stable/4027645. Accessed 30 July, 2017
2. Taylor, Michael A, and Hugh S Torrens. "An anonymous account of Mary Anning (1799–1847), fossil collector of Lyme Regis, Dorset, England, published in all the year round in 1865, and its attribution to Henry Stuart Fagan (1827–1890), schoolmaster, parson and author". *Proceedings of the Dorset Natural History & Archaeological Society* 135, 2014, Dorset Natural History and Archaeological Society: 72
3. Torrens, Hugh. "Presidential address: Mary Anning (1799–1847) of Lyme; 'the greatest fossilist the world ever knew'". *The British Journal for the History of Science* 28.3, 1995: 257–84, www.jstor.org/stable/4027645. Accessed 30 July, 2017
4. www.royalcollection.org.uk/collection/themes//maria-merians-butterflies/the-queens-gallery-buckingham-palace/branch-of-pomelo-with-green-banded-urania-moth. Accessed 23 July, 2017
5. www.theguardian.com/artanddesign/2016/apr/01/flora-fauna-and-fortitude-the-extraordinary-mission-of-maria-sibylla-merian#img-4. Accessed 23 July, 2017
6. Pieters, Florence F J M, and Diny Winthagen. "Maria Sibylla Merian, naturalist and artist (1647–1717): a commemoration on the occasion of the 350th anniversary of her birth". *Archives of natural history* 26.1, 1999: 1–18.
7. www.nationalgeographic.com/magazine/1970/01/mountain-gorillas-study-dian-fossey-virunga/

8. Ibid.
9. Ibid.
10. Montgomery, Sy. *Walking with the Great Apes: Jane Goodall, Dian Fossey, Biruté Galdikas*, Chelsea Green Publishing, 2009: 158.
11. Oakes, Elizabeth H. *Encyclopedia of World Scientists*, Infobase Publishing, 2007: 244.
12. www.un.org/en/sections/un-charter/un-charter-full-text/. Accessed 12 July, 2017
13. apnews.com/049889e630b7482 29887b91c8f21e3d2/researchers-latin-american-women-got-women-un-charter. Accessed 12 July, 2017
14. www.ipsnews.net/2016/09/how-latin-american-women-fought-for-womens-rights-in-the-un-charter/. Accessed 22 July, 2017
15. Kennedy, J P. "Ber tha Lutz, 1894–1976", *Copeia*, 1977: 209.
16. Hahner, June Edith. *Emancipating the Female Sex: The Struggle for Women's Rights in Brazil, 1850–1940*, Duke University Press, 1990: 149.
17. www.ipsnews.net/2016/09/how-latin-american-women-fought-for-womens-rights-in-the-un-charter/. Accessed 22 July, 2017
18. Vail, Anna Murray. "Jane Colden, an early New York botanist". *Torreya* 7.2, 1907: 21–34, www.jstor.org/stable/40594571. Accessed 1 September, 2017
19. Smith, Beatrice Scheer. "Jane Colden (1724–1766) and her botanic manuscript". *American Journal of Botany*, 1988): 1093, www.jstor.org/stable/2443778 Accessed 1 September, 2017
20. Harrison, Mary. "Jane Colden: colonial American botanist". *Arnoldia* 55.2, 1995: 25.
21. Smith, Beatrice Scheer. "Jane Colden (1724–1766) and her botanic manuscript". *American Journal of Botany*, 1988: 1091, www.jstor.org/stable/2443778. Accessed 1 September, 2017
22. www.estherlederberg.com/Oparin/EML%20Interview%20 p2.html. Accessed 24 September, 2017
23. Ibid.
24. Bonta, Marcia (ed.). *American Women Afield: Writings by Pioneering Women Naturalists*, Vol. 20, Texas A&M University Press, 1995: 136.
25. Ibid.: 147.
26. Ibid.: 138.

27. www.nobelprize.org/nobel_prizes/peace/laureates/2004/maathai-lecture-text.html. Accessed 23 July, 2017
28. Vidal, John. "Wangari Maathai obituary" in *Guardian* (26 September, 2011). Available at: www.theguardian.com/world/2011/sep/26/wangari-maathai. Accessed 23 July, 2017
29. Perlez, Jane. "Nairobi Journal; Skyscraper's Enemy Draws a Daily Dose of Scorn" in *New York Times* (6 December, 1989). Available at: www.nytimes.com/1989/12/06/world/nairobi-journal-skyscraper-s-enemy-draws-a-daily-dose-of-scorn.html. Accessed 23 July, 2017
30. www.theguardian.com/world/2011/sep/26/wangari-maathai. Accessed 23 July, 2017
31. www.nobelprize.org/nobel_prizes/peace/laureates/2004/maathai-lecture-text.html. Accessed 23 July, 2017
32. www.theguardian.com/environment/2009/may/30/africa-women-climate-change-wangari-maathai .Accessed 23 July, 2017

MEDICINE & PSYCHOLOGY

1. Parker, Holt. "Women doctors in Greece, Rome, and the Byzantine empire". *Women Healers and Physicians: Climbing a Long Hill*, 1997: 133.
2. Tsoucalas, Gregory, Antonis A Kousoulis, and George Androutsos. "Innovative surgical techniques of Aspasia, the early Greek gynecologist". *Surgical innovation* 19.3, 2012: 337.
3. Ibid.
4. wire.ama-assn.org/education/how-medical-specialties-vary-gender Accessed 26 September, 2017
5. Sander, Kathleen Waters. *Mary Elizabeth Garrett: Society and Philanthropy in the Gilded Age*, JHU Press, 2011: 154.
6. www.gmanetwork.com/news/news/specialreports/55128/pcij-dr-fe-del-mundo-a-woman-of-many-firsts/story/. Accessed 13 August, 2017
7. Ibid.
8. Ibid.
9. Ibid.
10. Emling, Shelley. *Marie Curie and Her Daughters: The Private Lives of Science's First Family*, St Martin's Press.

11. Ibid.
12. Ibid.
13. Ibid.
14. Gilmer, Penny J. "Irène Joliot-Curie, a Nobel laureate in artificial radioactivity". *Celebrating the 100th Anniversary of Madame Marie Sklodowska Curie's Nobel Prize in Chemistry*, 2011: 49.
15. www.jax.org/news-and-insights/jax-blog/2016/november/women-in-science-jane-wright. Accessed 27 July, 2017
16. Wright, Jane C. "Cancer chemotherapy: past, present, and future – part I". *Journal of the National Medical Association* 76.8, 1984: 773.
17. Weber, Bruce. "Jane Wright, Oncology Pioneer, Dies at 93" in *New York Times*, 2 March, 2013
18. "Interview with Ruby Hirose, 1924, Stanford Survey on Race Relations 1924–1927", Box 27, Item 159.
19. Hinnershitz, Stephanie. *Race, Religion, and Civil Rights: Asian Students on the West Coast, 1900–1968*, Rutgers University Press, 2015: 49.
20. Akagi, Roy Hidemichi. *The Second Generation Problem: Some Suggestions Toward its Solution*, No. 1, Japanese Students' Christian Association in North America, 1926: 10.
21. Ibid.: 40
22. Sohonie, K. "Opportunities for women scientists in India", in Richter, D (ed.). *Women Scientists: The Road to Liberation*, Palgrave, 1982: 14.
23. Gupta, Arvind. *Bright sparks: inspiring Indian scientists from the past*, Indian National Science Academy, 2009: 114-118.
24. Ibid.: 116.
25. Mitra, Anirban. "The life and times of Kamala Bhagvat Sohonie". *Resonance* 21.4, 2016: 307.
26. www.collectorsweekly.com/articles/getting-it-on-the-covert-history-of-the-american-condom/. Accessed 6 September, 2017
27. www.nyu.edu/projects/sanger/webedition/app/documents/show.php?sangerDoc=420004. xml. Accessed 6 September, 2017
28. www.nyu.edu/projects/sanger/webedition/app/documents/show.php?sangerDoc=101919. xml. Accessed 6 September, 2017
29. Ibid.
30. www.nyu.edu/projects/sanger/documents/this_i_believe.php. Accessed 6 September, 2017

31. Ibid.
32. www.nobelprize.org/nobel_
    prizes/medicine/laureates/1988/
    elion-bio.html.
    Accessed 20 August, 2017
33. Elion, Gertrude B. "The quest
    for a cure". *Annual Review of
    Pharmacology and Toxicology* 33.1,
    1993: 22.
34. Avery, Mary Ellen. "Gertrude
    Belle Elion. 23 January 1918 – 21
    February 1999", *Biographical
    Memoirs* 78, 2008.
35. www.nobelprize.org/nobel_
    prizes/medicine/laureates/1988/
    elion-bio.html.
    Accessed 20 August, 2017
36. www.nobelprize.org/nobel_
    prizes/medicine/laureates/1988/
    elion-bio.html.
    Accessed 20 August, 2017
37. Ingram, Robert A, et al.
    "Tributes to Gertrude Elion".
    The Oncologist 4.2, 1999: 0i–6a.
    Accessed 20 August, 2017
38. Avery, Mary Ellen. "Gertrude
    Belle Elion. 23 January 1918 – 21
    February 1999", *Biographical
    Memoirs* 78, 2008: 25.
39. Wilcox, Joyce. "The face
    of women's health: Helen
    Rodriguez-Trias". *American
    Journal of Public Health* 92.4,
    2002: 567.
40. Ibid.: 566
41. Ketenjian, Tanya. "Helen
    Rodriguez-Trias" in ed. Eldridge,
    Laura and Seaman, Barbara.
    *Voices of the Women's Health
    Movement* 1, Seven Stories Press,
    2012.
42. Ibid.
43. Ibid.
44. Ibid.
45. www.nytimes.com/2004/
    08/15/health/dr-kblerross-who-
    changed-perspectives-on-death-
    dies-at-78.html?_r=0.
    Accessed 7 August, 2017
46. Ibid.
47. Ibid.
48. Ibid.
49. Kubler-Ross, Elisabeth. "What
    is it like to be dying?". *The
    American Journal of Nursing*
    71.1, 1971: 54–62, www.jstor.
    org/stable/3421555. Accessed
    7 August, 2017
50. Ibid.: 56
51. Kubler-Ross, Elisabeth. *Death:
    The Final Stage*. Simon &
    Schuster, 1975: 1.
52. Silverman, Linda Kreger. "It all
    began with Leta Hollingworth:
    the story of giftedness in
    women". *Journal for the*

Education of the Gifted 12.2,
    1989: 88.
53. Ludy T Benjamin, Jr. "The
    pioneering work of Leta
    Hollingworth in the psychology
    of women". *Nebraska History* 56,
    1975: 494.
54. Silverman, Linda Kreger. "It all
    began with Leta Hollingworth:
    the story of giftedness in
    women". *Journal for the
    Education of the Gifted* 12.2,
    1989: 87.
55. Ludy T Benjamin, Jr. "The
    pioneering work of Leta
    Hollingworth in the psychology
    of women", *Nebraska History* 56,
    1975: 494.
56. Ibid.: 501.
57. Silverman, Linda Kreger. "It all
    began with Leta Hollingworth:
    the story of giftedness in
    women". *Journal for the
    Education of the Gifted* 12.2,
    1989: 90.

ELEMENTS & GENETICS

1. www.nature.com/scitable/
   topicpage/nettie-stevens-
   a-discoverer-of-sex-
   chromosomes-6580266 Accessed
   29 August, 2017
2. Mittwoch, Ursula. "Erroneous
   theories of sex determination".
   Journal of Medical Genetics 22.3,
   1985: 167.
3. Brush, Stephen G. "Nettie M.
   Stevens and the discovery of sex
   determination by chromosomes".
   Isis 69.2, 1978: 171, www.jstor.
   org/stable/230427.
   Accessed 29 August, 2017
4. Ibid.
5. Ibid.: 167
6. Van Tiggelen, Brigitte, and
   Annette Lykknes. "Ida and Walter
   Noddack through better and
   worse: an *Arbeitsgemeinschaft* in
   chemistry", in Lykknes A., Opitz D.,
   and Van Tiggelen B. (eds). *For
   Better or For Worse? Collaborative
   Couples in the Sciences*, Science
   Networks. Historical Studies,
   Vol. 44, Springer, 2012: 108.
7. Habashi, Fathi. "Ida Noddack:
   proposer of nuclear fission", in
   Rayner-Canham, Marelene F,
   and Geoffrey W Rayner-Canham.
   *A Devotion to Their Science:
   Pioneer Women of Radioactivity*,
   McGill-Queen's University Press,
   1997: 180.
8. Ibid.:221.
9. Ibid.
10. Watson, James. *The Double*

Helix, Orion, 2012.
11. profiles.nlm.nih.gov/ps/
    retrieve/Narrative/KR/p-nid/183
    Accessed 27 August, 2017
12. Elkin, Lynne Osman. "Rosalind
    Franklin and the double helix".
    Physics Today 56.3, 2003: 42.
13. Ibid.: 45.
14. profiles.nlm.nih.gov/ps/
    retrieve/Narrative/KR/p-nid/187
15. Watson, James. *The Double
    Helix*, Orion, 2012.
16. Ibid.
17. Ibid.
18. www.scientificamerican.com/
    article/finding-the-good-rita-levi-
    montalcini/.
    Accessed 28 August, 2017
19 www.independent.co.uk/news/
    science/is-this-the-secret-of-
    eternal-life-1674005.html.
    Accessed 28 August, 2017
20. www.nobelprize.org/nobel_
    prizes/medicine/laureates/1986/
    levi-montalcini-bio.html.
    Accessed 28 August, 2017
21. www.nature.com/news/
    2009/090401/full/458564a.html.
    Accessed 28 August, 2017

PHYSICS & CHEMISTRY

1. Chiang, Tsai-Chien. *Madame Wu
   Chien-Shiung: The First Lady of
   Physics Research*, World Scientific,
   2013: 116.
2. Ibid.: 90.
3. Ibid.: 98.
4. Ibid.: 141.
5. Ibid.: 147.
6. blogs.scientificamerican.com/
   guest-blog/channeling-ada-
   lovelace-chien-shiung-wu-
   courageous-hero-of-physics/.
   Accessed 19 August, 2017
7. Sime, Ruth Lewin. "Lise Meitner
   and the discovery of fission"
   Journal of Chemical Education,
   *Reflections on Nuclear Fission
   At the Half Century* 66:5,
   May 1989: 373.
8. Sime, Ruth Lewin. "Lise Meitner's
   escape from Germany". *American
   Journal of Physics* 58.3,1990: 266.
9. Ibid.:263
10. Meitner, Lise. "Lise Meitner
    looks back". *Advancement of
    Science* 21, 1964: 36.
11. Ibid.:12.
12. Sime, Ruth Lewin. "Lise Meitner
    and the discovery of fission",
    Journal of Chemical Education 66,
    1989: 373.
13. Ibid.
14. Ibid.
15. Sime, Ruth Lewin. Lise Meitner:

A Life in Physics, Vol. 11, University of California Press, 1996: 327.
16. Julie, Des. *The Madame Curie Complex: The Hidden History of Women in Science*, The Feminist Press at CUNY, 2010: 137
17. manhattanprojectvoices.org/oral-histories/leona-marshall-libbys-interview. Accessed 19 August, 2017
18. Ibid.
19. Findlen, Paula. "Science as a career in Enlightenment Italy: the strategies of Laura Bassi". *Isis* 84.3, 1993: 451, www.jstor.org/stable/235642. Accessed 12 September, 2017
20. Elena, Alberto. "'In lode della filosofessa di Bologna': an introduction to Laura Bassi". *Isis* 82.3, 1991: 510–18, www.jstor.org/stable/233228. Accessed 12 September, 2017
21. Cieślak-Golonka, Maria, and Bruno Morten. "The women scientists of Bologna: eighteenth-century Bologna provided a rare liberal environment in which brilliant women could flourish". *American Scientist* 88.1, 2000: 70, www.jstor.org/stable/27857965. Accessed 12 September, 2017
22. Findlen, Paula. "Laura Bassi and the city of learning". *Physics World* 26.09, 2013: 30.
23. Findlen, Paula. "Science as a career in Enlightenment Italy: the strategies of Laura Bassi". *Isis* 84.3, 1993: 455, www.jstor.org/stable/235642. Accessed 12 September, 2017
24. Findlen, Paula. "Laura Bassi and the city of learning". *Physics World* 26.9, 2013: 30.
25. Elena, Alberto. "'In lode della filosofessa di Bologna': an introduction to Laura Bassi". *Isis* 82.3, 1991: 513, www.jstor.org/stable/233228. Accessed 12 September, 2017
26. Findlen, Paula "Laura Bassi and the city of learning" *Physics World* 26.9, 2013:33
27. Ferry, Georgina. *Dorothy Hodgkin: A Life*, Bloomsbury Academic, 2014: 2.
28. Ibid.: 65.
29. www.independent.co.uk/news/people/obituary-professor-dorothy-hodgkin-1373624.html. Accessed 29 August, 2017
30. www.nobelprize.org/nobel_prizes/chemistry/laureates/1964/hodgkin-lecture.pdf. Accessed 29 August, 2017

MATHEMATICS

1. Watts, Edward J. *Hypatia* Oxford University Press, 2017: 15
2. Watts, Edward J. *City and School in Late Antique Athens and Alexandria*, Vol. 41, University of California Press, 2008: 187.
3. www.stoa.org/sol-bin/search.pl?login=guest&enlogin=guest&db=REAL&field=adlerhw_gr&searchstr=upsilon,166. Accessed 12 July, 2017
4. Watts, Edward J. *Hypatia*. Oxford University Press, 2017: 75.
5. Zinsser, Judith P. *Emilie Du Châtelet: Daring Genius of the Enlightenment*, Penguin, 2007: 54.
6. faculty.humanities.uci.edu/bjbecker/RevoltingIdeas/emilie.html. Accessed 6 September, 2017
7. Hagengruber, Ruth. *Emilie du Châtelet between Leibniz and Newton*, Springer, 2012: 184.
8. Steiner, George. "Machines and the man", *Sunday Times* (London, 23 October, 1983)
9. www.telegraph.co.uk/history/world-war-two/11323312/Bletchley-the-womens-story.html. Accessed 29 July, 2017
10. Smith, Michael. *The Debs of Bletchley Park and Other Stories*, Aurum Press Ltd, 2015: 172.
11. Ibid.: 187.
12. Ibid.: 181.
13. Ibid.: 154.
14. Ibid.: 236
15. Dunlop, Tessa. *The Bletchley Girls: War, Secrecy, Love and Loss: The Women of Bletchley Park Tell Their Story*, Hodder & Stoughton, 2015.
16. arxiv.org/pdf/hep-th/9411110.pdf. Accessed 12 July, 2017
17. Ibid.: 21
18. Ibid.
19. Angier, Natalie. "The mighty mathematician you've never heard of". *New York Times* (26 March, 2012).
20. Kimberling, Clark H. "Emmy Noether". *The American Mathematical Monthly* 79.2, 1972: 137.
21. Kovalevskaya, Sofya. *A Russian Childhood*, Springer Science & Business Media, 2013: 57.
22. Ibid.: 77.
23. Ibid.: 170.
24. Swaby, Rachel. *Headstrong: 52 Women who Changed Science – and the World*, Crown/Archetype, 2015, Broadway Books.
25. Kovalevskaya, Sofya. *A Russian*

Childhood, Springer Science & Business Media, 2013: 23.
26. Swaby, Rachel. *Headstrong: 52 Women who Changed Science – and the World*, Crown/Archetype, 2015, Broadway Books.
27. Ibid.
28. Kovalevskaya, Sofya. *A Russian Childhood*, Springer Science & Business Media, 2013: 35.
29. Ibid:172.
30. Dalmédico, A D. "Sophie Germain". *Scientific American* 265.6, 1991: 119.
31. Ibid.
32. www.brainpickings.org/2017/02/22/sophie-germain-gauss/. Accessed 8 August, 2017
33. Ibid.

TECHNOLOGY & INVENTIONS

1. Patai, Raphael. *The Jewish Alchemists: A History and Source Book*, Princeton University Press, 2014: 5
2. Ibid.: 70.
3. Patai, Raphael. "Maria the Jewess–founding mother of alchemy", *Ambix*, Nov 29(3), 1982: 177.
4. Jeffrey, Laura S. *Amazing American Inventors of the 20th Century*, Enslow Publishers, Inc., 2013: 9.
5. Ibid.
6. Ibid.: 32.
7. Blashfield, Jean F. *Women Inventors* 4. Capstone, 1996: 35.
8. Mason, Joan. "Hertha Ayrton (1854–1923) and the admission of women to the Royal Society of London". *Notes and Records of the Royal Society of London* 45.2, 1991: 169, www.jstor.org/stable/531699. Accessed 5 August, 2017
9. Swaby, Rachel. *Headstrong: 52 Women who Changed Science – and the World*, Crown/Archetype, 2015, Broadway books
10. Mason, Joan. "Hertha Ayrton (1854–1923) and the admission of women to the Royal Society of London". *Notes and Records of the Royal Society of London* 45.2 , 1991: 211, www.jstor.org/stable/531699. Accessed 5 August, 2017
11. Ibid.:216.
12. www.atlasobscura.com/places/grace-hoppers-bug. Accessed 11 July, 2017
13. Grace Hopper on The Letterman Show: youtu.be/1-vcErOPofQ?t=1m54s, www.

wired.com/2014/10/grace-hopper-letterman/. Accessed 11 July, 2017
14. www.bbc.co.uk/news/business-38677721. Accessed 11 July, 2017
15. crgis.ndc.nasa.gov/crgis/images/d/d3/MannBio.pdf. Accessed 11 September, 2017
16. Shetterly, Margot Lee. *Hidden Figures: The Untold Story of the African American Women Who Helped Win the Space Race,* HarperCollins Publishers, 2016: 217.
17. St. Martin, Victoria. "Hidden no more: Katherine Johnson, a black NASA pioneer, finds acclaim at 98" in *Washington Post* (27 January, 2017).
18. Le Hir, Pierre. "Rose Dieng, en cerveau sans frontières" in *Le Monde* (11 January, 2006).
19. Ibid.
20. Ibid.
21. Marshal, Jane. "SENEGAL-FRANCE: Death of Web Pioneer" in *University World News* (20 July, 2008).
22. Ibid.
23. Markus, Julia. *Lady Byron and Her Daughters,* WW Norton & Company, 2015: 26.
24. Markus, Julia. *Lady Byron and Her Daughters,* WW Norton & Company, 2015: 83.
25. Augustus De Morgan on the mathematics of Ada Lovelace: findingada.com/about/ada-lovelace-links/. Accessed 11 July, 2017
26. Faraday, Michael. *The Correspondence of Michael Faraday: 1841-1848,* IET, 1996: 164.
27. Essinger, James. *Ada's Algorithm: How Lord Byron's Daughter Ada Lovelace Launched the Digital Age,* Gibson Square Books, 2013: Chapter 14.
28. Bowden, BV ed. *Faster Than Thought (A Symposium on Digital Computing Machines),* Sir Isaac Pitman & Sons Ltd, 1953: vii.

THE EARTH & THE UNIVERSE

The Harvard Computers (1881–1919)

Sobel, Dava. *The Glass Universe: The Hidden History of the Women Who Took the Measure of the Stars,* HarperCollins Publishers, 2017

www.bostonglobe.com/lifestyle/2017/08/10/women-computers-held-stars-their-hands/qfLYwpsNZdFNHyiY2igPNJ/story.html. Accessed 20 August, 2017

www.smithsonianmag.com/history/the-women-who-mapped-the-universe-and-still-couldnt-get-any-respect-9287444/. Accessed 20 August, 2017

www.space.com/34675-harvard-computers.html. Accessed 20 August, 2017

www.spectator.co.uk/2017/01/the-harvard-housewives-who-measured-the-heavens/. Accessed 20 August, 2017

www.theatlantic.com/science/archive/2016/12/the-women-computers-who-measured-the-stars/509231/. Accessed 20 August, 2017

Inge Lehmann (1888–1981)

Bolt, Bruce A "Inge Lehmann. 13 May 1888 – 21 February 1993", 1997: 287–301

Lehmann, Inge. "Seismology in the days of old". *Eos, Transactions American Geophysical Union* 68.3, 1987: 33–5

Williams, C A, J A Hudson, and B S Jeffreys. "Inge Lehmann (13 May 1888–1993)". *Quarterly Journal of the Royal Astronomical Society* 35, 1994: 231–4

www.amnh.org/explore/resource-collections/earth-inside-and-out/inge-lehmann-discoverer-of-the-earth-s-inner-core/. Accessed 31 August, 2017

www.vox.com/2015/5/13/8595157/inge-lehmann. Accessed 31 August, 2017

Cecilia Payne-Gaposchkin (1900–1979)

Haramundanis, Katherine (ed.). *Cecilia Payne-Gaposchkin: An Autobiography and Other Recollections*, Cambridge University Press, 1996

Wayman, Patrick A. "Cecilia Payne-Gapsochkin: astronomer extraordinaire". *Astronomy & Geophysics* 43. 1 (1 February 2002): 1.27–1.29, doi.org/10.1046/j.1468-4004.2002.43127.x. Accessed 1 September, 2017

www.aps.org/publications/apsnews/201501/physicshistory.cfm#1. Accessed 1 September, 2017

Wang Zhenyi (1768–1797)

Bernardi, Gabriella. *The Unforgotten Sisters: Female Astronomers and Scientists Before Caroline Herschel*, Springer, 2016

Ko, Dorothy. "Pursuing talent and virtue: education and women's culture in seventeenth- and eighteenth-century China". *Late Imperial China* 13.1, 1992: 9–39

Peterson, Barbara Bennett. *Notable Women of China: Shang Dynasty to the Early Twentieth Century*, Routledge, 2016

Wiles, Sue. *Biographical Dictionary of Chinese Women: The Qing Period, 1644–1911*, No. 10, M E Sharpe, 1998

Annie Scott Dill Maunder (1868–1947)

Bruck, Mary T. "ALICE Everett and Annie Russell Maunder torch bearing women astronomers". *Irish Astronomical Journal* 21, 1994: 280–391

Bruck, Mary T. "Lady computers at Greenwich in the early 1890s". *Quarterly Journal of the Royal Astronomical Society* 36 , 1995: 83

Evershed, M A. "Obituary notices:– Maunder, Annie Scott Dill". *Monthly Notices of the Royal Astronomical Society* 108, 1948: 48

Maunder, Annie S D, and E Walter. *The Heavens and Their Story.*, R Culley, 1908, Introduction

www.bbc.co.uk/news/science-environment-37496677. Accessed 24 August, 2017

Ruby Payne-Scott (1912–1981)

www.abc.net.au/radionational/programs/scienceshow/ruby-payne-scott---radio-astronomer/3403336#transcript. Accessed 27 August, 2017

cpsu-csiro.org.au/2012/05/29/star-achiever-celebrating-100-years-of-ruby-payne-scott/. Accessed 27 August, 2017

www.naa.gov.au/collection/snapshots/find-of-the-month/2009-march.aspx. Accessed 27 August, 2017

BIOLOGY & NATURAL SCIENCES

Mary Anning (1799–1847)

Taylor, Michael A, and Hugh S Torrens. "An account of Mary Anning (1799–1847), fossil collector of Lyme Regis, Dorset, England, published by Henry Rowland Brown (1837–1921) in the second edition (1859) of beauties of Lyme Regis". *Proceedings of the Dorset Natural History & Archaeological Society* 135, 2014, Dorset Natural History and Archaeological Society: 63–70

Taylor, Michael A, and Hugh S Torrens. "An anonymous account of Mary Anning (1799–1847), fossil collector of Lyme Regis, Dorset, England, published in all the year round in 1865, and its attribution to Henry Stuart Fagan (1827–1890), schoolmaster, parson and author". *Proceedings of the Dorset Natural History & Archaeological Society* 135, 2014, Dorset Natural History and Archaeological Society: 71–85

Torrens, Hugh. "Presidential address: Mary Anning (1799–1847) of Lyme; 'the greatest fossilist the world ever knew'". *The British Journal for the History of Science* 28.3, 1995: 257–84, www.jstor.org/stable/4027645. Accessed 30 July, 2017

Maria Sibylla Merian (1647–1717)

public.gettysburg.edu/~ketherid/Merian%201st%20ecologist.pdf. Accessed 23 July, 2017

pure.uva.nl/ws/files/956970/80552_327018.pdf. Accessed 23 July, 2017

www.theatlantic.com/science/archive/2016/01/the-woman-who-made-science-beautiful/424620/. Accessed 23 July, 2017

www.theguardian.com/artanddesign/2016/apr/01/flora-fauna-and-fortitude-the-extraordinary-mission-of-maria-sibylla-merian#img-4. Accessed 23 July, 2017

Dian Fossey (1932–1985)

Montgomery, Sy. Walking with the Great Apes: Jane Goodall, Dian Fossey, Biruté Galdikas, Chelsea Green Publishing, 2009. Accessed 16 July, 2017

Oakes, Elizabeth H. *Encyclopedia of World Scientists*. Infobase Publishing, 2007

www.bbc.co.uk/earth/story/20151226-the-woman-who-gave-her-life-to-save-the-gorillas. Accessed 16 July, 2017

www.vanityfair.com/style/1986/09/fatal-obsession-198609. Accessed 16 July, 2017

Bertha Lutz (1894–1976)

Hahner, June Edith. *Emancipating the Female Sex: The Struggle for Women's Rights in Brazil, 1850–1940*, Duke University Press, 1990

Kennedy, J P. "Bertha Lutz, 1894–1976". *Copeia* 1, 1977: 208–9

Rachum, Ilan. "Feminism, woman suffrage, and national politics in Brazil: 1922–1937". *Luso-Brazilian Review* 14.1, 1977: 118–34

americasouthandnorth.wordpress.com/2013/05/12/get-to-know-a-brazilian-bertha-lutz-2/. Accessed 22 July, 2017

apnews.com/049889e630b74822
9887b91c8f21e3d2/researchers-
latin-american-women-got-
women-un-charter.
Accessed 22 July, 2017

www.ipsnews.net/2016/09/how-
latin-american-women-fought-for-
womens-rights-in-the-un-charter/.
Accessed 22 July, 2017

thenewinquiry.com/blog/feminism-
fascism-and-frogs-the-case-of-
bertha-lutz-at-the-united-nations/.
Accessed 22 July, 2017

www.un-ngls.org/images/
multilateralism/UnfinishedStory.
pdf. Accessed 22 July, 2017

Jane Colden (1724–1766)

Harrison, Mary. "Jane Colden:
colonial American botanist".
Arnoldia 55.2, 1995: 19–26

Smith, Beatrice Scheer. "Jane Colden
(1724–1766) and her botanic
manuscript". *American Journal
of Botany*, 1988: 1090–6,
www.jstor.org/stable/2443778

Vail, Anna Murray. "Jane Colden,
an early New York botanist".
Torreya 7.2, 1907: 21–34,
www.jstor.org/stable/40594571.
Accessed 1 September, 2017

Wilson, Joan Hoff. "Dancing dogs
of the colonial period: women
scientists". *Early American
Literature* 7.3, 1973: 225–35,
www.jstor.org/stable/25070582
Accessed 1 September, 2017

Esther Lederberg (1922–2006)

www.estherlederberg.com/
Anecdotes.html.
Accessed 24 September, 2017

www.jax.org/news-and-insights/jax-
blog/2016/december/invisible-
esther.
Accessed 24 September, 2017

news.stanford.edu/news/2006/
november29/med-esther-
112906.html.
Accessed 24 September, 2017

www.theguardian.com/
science/2006/dec/13/obituaries.
guardianobituaries.
Accessed 24 September, 2017

www.thelancet.com/pdfs/journals/
lancet/PIIS0140673606698802.
pdf. Accessed 24 September, 2017

Ynés Mexía (1870–1938)

Bonta, Marcia (ed.). *American
Women Afield: Writings by
Pioneering Women Naturalists*,
Vol. 20, Texas A&M University
Press, 1995

Bracelin, H P. "Ynes Mexia".
Madroño 4.8, 1938: 273–5

www.calacademy.org/
blogs/from-the-stacks/archives-
unboxed-ynes-mexia.
Accessed 20 July, 2017

Wangari Maathai (1940–2011)

www.nobelprize.org/nobel_prizes/
peace/laureates/2004/maathai-
lecture-text.html.
Accessed 23 July, 2017

www.nytimes.com/1989/12/06/
world/nairobi-journal-skyscraper-
s-enemy-draws-a-daily-dose-of-
scorn.html. Accessed 23 July, 2017

www.theguardian.com/world/2011/
sep/26/wangari-maathai.
Accessed 23 July, 2017

MEDICINE & PSYCHOLOGY

Aspasia (c.4th century AD)

Gregory, Tsoucalas, and Sgantzos
Markos. "Aspasia and Cleopatra
Metrodora, two majestic female
physician-surgeons in the early
Byzantine era". *Journal of
Universal Surgery*, 2016

Parker, Holt. "Women doctors in
Greece, Rome, and the Byzantine
empire". *Women Healers and
Physicians: Climbing a Long Hill*,
1997: 131–50

Ricci, James Vincent. "The
development of gynaecological
surgery and instruments". Norman
Publishing, 1940: 31 onward

Riddle, John M. *Contraception and
Abortion from the Ancient World
to the Renaissance*. Harvard
University Press, 1994: 97 onward

Fe del Mundo (1912–2011)

curiosity.com/topics/fe-del-mundo/.
Accessed 13 August, 2017

www.gmanetwork.com/news/news/
specialreports/55128/pcij-dr-fe-
del-mundo-a-woman-of-many-
firsts/story/.
Accessed 13 August, 2017

newsinfo.inquirer.net/37419/
beautiful-life-as-doctor-to-
generations-of-kids-99.
Accessed 13 August, 2017

Irène Joliot-Curie (1897–1956)

Emling, Shelley. *Marie Curie and
Her Daughters: The Private Lives of
Science's First Family*, St Martin's
Press, 2012

Gilmer, Penny J. "Irène Joliot-Curie,
a Nobel laureate in artificial
radioactivity". *Celebrating the
100th Anniversary of Madame
Marie Sklodowska Curie's Nobel
Prize in Chemistry*, 2011: 41–57

Jane C Wright (1919–2013)

www.bmj.com/content/346/bmj.
f2902. Accessed 27 July, 2017

www.aacr.org/Membership/
Shared%20Documents/Jane_
Cooke_Wright____2141F3.pdf.
Accessed 27 July, 2017

www.ascopost.com/issues/may-15-
2014/asco-cofounder-jane-cooke-
wright-md-defied-racialgender-
barriers-and-helped-usher-in-the-
modern-age-of-chemotherapy/.
Accessed 28 July, 2017

cfmedicine.nlm.nih.gov/physicians/
biography_336.html.
Accessed 28 July, 2017

www.jax.org/news-and-insights/
jax-blog/2016/november/women-
in-science-jane-wright.
Accessed 27 July, 2017

www.nytimes.com/2013/03/03/
health/jane-c-wright-pioneering-
oncologist-dies-at-93.html.
Accessed 27 July, 2017

thelancet.com/journals/lancet/
article/PIIS0140-6736(13)60874-
0/fulltext. Accessed 27 July, 2017

Ruby Hirose (1904–1960)

Akagi, Roy Hidemichi. *The Second Generation Problem: Some Suggestions Toward its Solution*, No. 1, Japanese Students' Christian Association in North America, 1926

Hinnershitz, Stephanie. *Race, Religion, and Civil Rights: Asian Students on the West Coast, 1900–1968*, Rutgers University Press, 2015

"Interview with Ruby Hirose, 1924, Stanford Survey on Race Relations 1924–1927", Box 27, Item 159

auburnpioneercemetery.net/ biographies/hirose.php#. WWidENPyuRt. Accessed 14 July, 2017

auburnpioneercemetery.net/ blog/2013/08/an-american-born-japanese-girl-scientist/. Accessed 14 July, 2017

energy.gov/articles/five-fast-facts-about-dr-ruby-hirose. Accessed 14 July, 2017

siarchives.si.edu/collections/ siris_arc_297429. Accessed 14 July, 2017

winsatnyu.wordpress. com/2015/04/09/ruby-hirose-1904-1960/. Accessed 14 July, 2017

Gertrude B Elion (1918–1999)

Avery, Mary Ellen. "Gertrude Belle Elion. 23 January 1918 – 21 February 1999" *Biographical Memoirs* 78, The National Academic Press, 2008: 161–8

Elion, Gertrude B. "The quest for a cure". *Annual Review of Pharmacology and Toxicology* 33.1, 1993: 1–25

Ingram, Robert A, et al. "Tributes to Gertrude Elion". *The Oncologist* 4.2, 1999: 0i–6a

www.nobelprize.org/nobel_prizes/ medicine/laureates/1988/elion-bio.html. Accessed 20 August, 2017

www.nytimes.com/1999/02/23/ us/gertrude-elion-drug-developer-dies-at-81.html. Accessed 20 August, 2017

Kamala Sohonie (1912–1998)

Dhuru, Vasumati. "The scientist lady", in Godbole, Rohini M (ed.). *Lilavati's Daughters: The Women Scientists of India*, Indian Academy of Sciences, 2008: 31–34

Gupta, Arvind. *Bright sparks: inspiring Indian scientists of the past*, Indian National Science Academy, 2009: 114–118

Mitra, Anirban. "The life and times of Kamala Bhagvat Sohonie". *Resonance* 21.4, 2016: 301–14

Margaret Sanger (1879–1966)

Lehfeldt, Hans. "Margaret Sanger 1883–1966". Journal of Sex Research 2.3, 1966: 154–6

Lehfeldt, Hans. "Margaret Sanger and the modern contraceptive techniques". *The Journal of Sex Research*, 1967: 253–5

www.collectorsweekly.com/articles/ getting-it-on-the-covert-history-of-the-american-condom/. Accessed 2 August, 2017

content.time.com/time/ subscriber/article/0,33009,988152, 00.html. Accessed 6 September, 2017

www.nytimes.com/2006/10/15/ opinion/nyregionopinions/15CIf eldt.html. Accessed 2 August, 2017

www.nyu.edu/projects/sanger/ aboutms/index.php. Accessed 2 August, 2017

www.nyu.edu/projects/sanger/ documents/this_i_believe.php. Accessed 2 August, 2017

www.nyu.edu/projects/ sanger/webedition/app/documents/ show.php?sangerDoc=101919. xml. Accessed 6 September, 2017

www.nyu.edu/projects/sanger/ webedition/app/documents/show. php?sangerDoc=420004.xml. Accessed 6 September, 2017

Helen Rodríguez-Trías (1929–2001)

Eldridge, Laura, and Barbara Seaman (eds). *Voices of the Women's Health Movement*, Vol. 1, Seven Stories Press, 2012

Newman, Laura. "Helen Rodriguez-Trias: public health activist who improved the quality of health care for women around the world". *British Medical Journal* 324.7331, 2002: 242

Wilcox, Joyce. "The face of women's health: Helen Rodriguez-Trias". *American Journal of Public Health* 92.4, 2002: 566–9

cfmedicine.nlm.nih.gov/physicians/ biography_273.html. Accessed 9 August, 2017

www.ncbi.nlm.nih.gov/pmc/articles/ PMC1122157/. Accessed 9 August, 2017

www.ourbodiesourselves.org/health-info/forced-sterilization/. Accessed 9 August, 2017

Elisabeth Kübler-Ross (1926–2004)

Kubler-Ross, Elisabeth. *Death: The Final Stage*. Simon & Schuster, 1975: 1

Kubler-Ross, Elisabeth. "What is it like to be dying?". *The American Journal of Nursing* 71.1, 1971: 54–62, www.jstor.org/ stable/3421555

www.newyorker.com/ magazine/2010/02/01/good-grief. Accessed 7 August, 2017

www.nytimes.com/ 2004/08/25/health/dr-kblerross-who-changed-perspectives-on-death-dies-at-78.html?_r=0. Accessed 7 August, 2017

www.nytimes.com/2004/ 08/26/us/elisabeth-kubler-ross-78-dies-psychiatrist-revolutionized-care-terminally-ill.html?_r=0. Accessed 7 August, 2017

www.theguardian.com/ society/2004/aug/31/ mentalhealth.guardianobituaries. Accessed 7 August, 2017

Leta Hollingworth (1886–1939)

Benjamin Jr, Ludy T. "The pioneering work of Leta Hollingworth in the psychology of women". *Nebraska History* 56, 1975: 493–505

Silverman, Linda Kreger. "It all began with Leta Hollingworth: the story of giftedness in women". *Journal for the Education of the Gifted* 12.2, 1989: 86–98

ELEMENTS & GENETICS

Nettie Stevens (1861–1912)

Brush, Stephen G. "Nettie M. Stevens and the discovery of sex determination by chromosomes". Isis 69.2, 1978: 163–72, www.jstor.org/stable/230427. Accessed 29 August, 2017

Mittwoch, Ursula. "Erroneous theories of sex determination". *Journal of Medical Genetics* 22.3, 1985: 164–70

Swaby, Rachel. Headstrong: 52 *Women who Changed Science – and the World*, Broadway Books, 2015

genestogenomes.org/nettie-stevens-sex-chromosomes-and-sexism/. Accessed 29 August, 2017

www.nature.com/scitable/topicpage/nettie-stevens-a-discoverer-of-sex-chromosomes-6580266. Accessed 29 August, 2017

Ida Noddack (1896–1978)

Habashi, Fathi. "Ida Noddack: proposer of nuclear fission", in Rayner-Canham, Marelene F, and Geoffrey W Rayner-Canham. *A Devotion to Their Science: Pioneer Women of Radioactivity*, McGill-Queen's University Press, 1997: 215–224

Santos, Gildo Magalhães. "A tale of oblivion: Ida Noddack and the 'universal abundance' of matter". *Notes and Records of the Royal Society of London* 68.4 2014: 373–89. www.ncbi.nlm.nih.gov/pmc/articles/PMC4213432/#FN2. Accessed 27 August, 2017

Van Tiggelen, Brigitte, and Annette Lykknes. "Ida and Walter Noddack through better and worse: an Arbeitsgemeinschaft in chemistry",

in Lykknes A., Opitz D., and Van Tiggelen B. (eds). *For Better or For Worse? Collaborative Couples in the Sciences*, Science Networks. Historical Studies, Vol. 44, Springer, 2012: 103–47

Rosalind Franklin (1920–1958)

Elkin, Lynne Osman. "Rosalind Franklin and the double helix". Physics Today 56.3, 2003: 42–8

Watson, James. *The Double Helix*. Orion, 2012

profiles.nlm.nih.gov/ps/retrieve/Narrative/KR/p-nid/183. Accessed 27 August, 2017

profiles.nlm.nih.gov/ps/retrieve/Narrative/KR/p-nid/187. Accessed 27 August, 2017

Rita Levi-Montalcini (1909–2012)

Swaby, Rachel. Headstrong: 52 *Women who Changed Science – and the World*, Broadway Books, 2015

www.independent.co.uk/news/science/is-this-the-secret-of-eternal-life-1674005.html. Accessed 28 August, 2017

www.nature.com/news/2009/090401/full/458564a.html. Accessed 28 August, 2017

www.nytimes.com/2012/12/31/science/dr-rita-levi-montalcini-a-revolutionary-in-the-study-of-the-brain-dies-at-103.html. Accessed 28 August, 2017

www.scientificamerican.com/article/finding-the-good-rita-levi-montalcini/. Accessed 28 August, 2017

www.theguardian.com/science/2012/dec/30/rita-levi-montalcini. Accessed 28 August, 2017

PHYSICS & CHEMISTRY

Tapputi (c.1200 BC)

Herzenberg, Caroline L. "Women in science during antiquity and the Middle Ages". *Interdisciplinary Science Reviews* 15.4, 1990: 294–7

Kass-Simon, Gabriele, Patricia Farnes, and Deborah Nash (eds). *Women of Science: Righting the Record*, Indiana University Press, 1993

Levey, Martin. "Babylonian chemistry: a study of Arabic and second millenium BC perfumery". *Osiris* 12 , 1956: 376–89

Levey, Martin. *Early Arabic Pharmacology: An Introduction Based on Ancient and Medieval Sources*, Brill Archive, 1973

Mitter, Swasti, and Sheila Rowbotham (eds). *Women Encounter Technology: Changing Patterns of Employment in the Third World*, Vol. 1, Psychology Press, 1997

Laura Bassi (1711–1778)

Cieślak-Golonka, Maria, and Bruno Morten. "The women scientists of Bologna: eighteenth-century Bologna provided a rare liberal environment in which brilliant women could flourish". *American Scientist* 88.1, 2000: 68–73, www.jstor.org/stable/27857965. Accessed 12 September, 2017

Elena, Alberto. "'In lode della filosofessa di Bologna': an introduction to Laura Bassi". *Isis* 82.3, 1991: 510–18, www.jstor.org/stable/233228. Accessed 12 September, 2017

Findlen, Paula. "Laura Bassi and the city of learning". *Physics World* 26.09, 2013: 30–34

Findlen, Paula. "Science as a career in Enlightenment Italy: the strategies of Laura Bassi". *Isis* 84.3, 1993: 441–69, www.jstor.org/stable/235642. Accessed 12 September, 2017

Lise Meitner (1878–1968)

Frisch, Otto Robert. "Lise Meitner. 1878–1968". *Biographical Memoirs of Fellows of the Royal Society* 16, 1970: 405–20

Meitner, Lise. "Lise Meitner looks back". *Advancement of Science* 21, 1964: 39–46

Sime, Ruth Lewin. Lise Meitner: A Life in Physics, Vol. 11, University of California Press, 1996

Sime, Ruth Lewin. "Lise Meitner and the discovery of fission" *Journal of Chemical Education* 66.5, 1989: 373–376

Sime, Ruth Lewin. "Lise Meitner's escape from Germany". *American Journal of Physics* 58.3, 1990: 262–7

Chien-Shiung Wu (1912–1997)

Chiang, Tsai-Chien. *Madame Wu Chien-Shiung: The First Lady of Physics Research*, World Scientific, 2013

Swaby, Rachel. *Headstrong: 52 Women who Changed Science-and the World*, Broadway Books, 2015

blogs.scientificamerican.com/guest-blog/channeling-ada-lovelace-chien-shiung-wu-courageous-hero-of-physics/. Accessed 19 August, 2017

www.nytimes.com/1997/02/18/us/chien-shiung-wu-84-dies-top-experimental-physicist.html. Accessed 19 August, 2017

time.com/4366137/chien-shiung-wu-history/. Accessed 19 August, 2017

Leona Woods Marshall Libby (1919–1986)

Julie, Des. *The Madame Curie Complex: The Hidden History of Women in Science*, The Feminist Press at CUNY, 2010

Ogilvie, Marilyn, and Joy Harvey. *The Biographical Dictionary of Women in Science: Pioneering Lives from Ancient Times to the Mid-20th Century*, Routledge, 2003: 788

articles.latimes.com/1986-11-13/local/me-24930_1_nuclear-reactor. Accessed 19 August, 2017

energy.gov/articles/history-women-energy-department. Accessed 19 August, 2017

manhattanprojectvoices.org/oral-histories/leona-marshall-libbys-interview. Accessed 19 August, 2017

matt.distort.org/docs/science%20history/WomenInTheManhattanProject.pdf. Accessed 19 August, 2017

www.nytimes.com/1979/09/30/archives/the-uranium-people.html?_r=0. Accessed 19 August, 2017

Dorothy Hodgkin (1910–1994)

Ferry, Georgina. *Dorothy Hodgkin: A Life*, Bloomsbury Publishing, 2014

www.independent.co.uk/news/people/obituary-professor-dorothy-hodgkin-1373624.html. Accessed 29 August, 2017

www.nobelprize.org/nobel_prizes/chemistry/laureates/1964/hodgkin-lecture.pdf. Accessed 29 August, 2017

www.theguardian.com/science/occams-corner/2014/jan/14/dorothy-hodgkin-year-of-crystallography. Accessed 29 August, 2017

MATHEMATICS

Hypatia of Alexandria (c.AD 355)

Mark, J J. "Hypatia of Alexandria", in *Ancient History Encyclopedia*, 2009, www.ancient.eu/Hypatia_of_Alexandria/. Accessed 12 July, 2017

The Suda, www.stoa.org/sol-bin/search.pl?login=guest&enlogin=guest&db=REAL&field=adler hw_gr&searchstr=upsilon,166. Accessed 12 July, 2017

Watts, Edward J. *Hypatia*, Oxford University Press, 2017

Zielinski, Sarah. "Hypatia, ancient Alexandria's great female scholar". Smithsonian (15 March 2010), www.smithsonianmag.com/history/hypatia-ancient-alexandrias-great-female-scholar-10942888/. Accessed 12 July, 2017

Émilie du Châtelet (1706–1749)

Osen, Lynn M. *Women in Mathematics*, MIT Press, 1975

Waithe, Mary Ellen (ed.). *A History of Women Philosophers: Vol. III: 1600–1900*, Springer Science & Business Media, 1991

Zinsser, Judith P. "Mentors, the Marquise Du Châtelet and historical memory". *Notes and Records of the Royal Society* 61.2, 2007: 89–108

www.aps.org/publications/apsnews/200812/physicshistory.cfm. Accessed 6 September, 2017

faculty.humanities.uci.edu/bjbecker/RevoltingIdeas/emilie.html. Accessed 6 September, 2017

www-groups.dcs.st-and.ac.uk/~history/Biographies/Chatelet.html. Accessed 6 September, 2017

www.pbs.org/wgbh/nova/physics/ancestors-einstein.html. Accessed 6 September, 2017

www.theguardian.com/science/2006/aug/04/peopleinscience.guardianweekly. Accessed 6 September, 2017

The Bletchleyettes

Dunlop, Tessa. *The Bletchley Girls: War, Secrecy, Love and Loss: The Women of Bletchley Park Tell Their Story*, Hodder & Stoughton, 2015

Smith, Michael. *The Debs of Bletchley Park and Other Stories*, Aurum Press Ltd, 2015

www.huffingtonpost.co.uk/2015/01/25/bletchley-park-enigma-female-codebreakers_n_6532856.html. Accessed 29 July, 2017

www.telegraph.co.uk/history/world-war-two/11323312/Bletchley-the-womens-story.html. Accessed 29 July, 2017

Emmy Noether (1882–1935)

Angier, Natalie. "The mighty mathematician wou've never heard ff". *New York Times* (26 March, 2012)

arxiv.org/pdf/hep-th/9411110.pdf. Accessed 12 July, 2017

Kimberling, Clark H. "Emmy Noether". *The American Mathematical Monthly* 79.2, 1972: 136–49

www-groups.dcs.st-and.ac.uk/
history/Obits2/Noether_Emmy_
Einstein.html.
Accessed 12 July, 2017

Sofia Kovalevskaya (1850–1891)

Kovalevskaya, Sofya. *A Russian
Childhood*, Springer Science &
Business Media, 2013

Swaby, Rachel. *Headstrong: 52
Women who Changed Science – and
the World*, Crown/Archetype,
Broadway Books, 2015

Sophie Germain (1776–1831)

Case, Bettye Anne, and Anne M
Leggett (eds). *Complexities:
Women in Mathematics*, Princeton
University Press, 2005

Dalmédico, A D. "Sophie Germain".
Scientific American 265.6, 1991:
116–23

Musielak, Dora E. *Prime Mystery:
The Life and Mathematics of Sophie
Germain*, Authorhouse, 2015

www.brainpickings.
org/2017/02/22/sophie-germain-
gauss/. Accessed 8 August, 2017

www.thoughtco.com/sophie-
germain-biography-3530360.
Accessed: 8 August, 2017

TECHNOLOGY & INVENTIONS

**Maria the Jewess
(c.AD 2nd–3rd century)**

Offereins, Marianne. "Maria the
Jewess". *European Women in
Chemistry*, 2011: 1–3

Patai, Raphael. *The Jewish
Alchemists: A History and Source
Book*, Princeton University Press,
2014

Van der Horst, Pieter W. "Maria
Alchemista, the first female Jewish
author" in *Zutot*, 2001, Springer,
2002: 44–7

**Mary Beatrice Davidson Kenner
(1912–2006)**

Blashfield, Jean F. *Women Inventors*,
Vol. 4, Capstone, 1996: 11

Jeffrey, Laura S. *Amazing American
Inventors of the 20th Century*,
Enslow Publishers, Inc., 2013

Hertha Ayrton (1885–1923)

Mason, Joan. "Hertha Ayrton
(1854–1923) and the admission
of women to the Royal Society
of London". *Notes and Records of
the Royal Society of London* 45. 2,
1991: 201–20,
www.jstor.org/stable/531699.
Accessed 5 August, 2017

Swaby, Rachel. *Headstrong: 52
Women who Changed Science – and
the World*, Crown/Archetype,
Broadway Books, 2015

jwa.org/encyclopedia/article/ayrton-
hertha-marks.
Accessed 5 August, 2017

www.theiet.org/resources/library/
archives/biographies/ayrtonh.cfm.
Accessed 5 August, 2017

**Admiral Grace Hopper
(1906–1992)**

Beyer, Kurt W. *Grace Hopper and the
Invention of the Information Age*,
BookBaby, 2015

www.atlasobscura.com/places/
grace-hoppers-bug.
Accessed 11 July, 2017

www.bbc.co.uk/news/
business-38677721.
Accessed 11 July, 2017

www.wired.com/2014/10/grace-
hopper-letterman/.
Accessed 11 July, 2017

The West Computers (1940s–60s)

Shetterly, Margot Lee. *Hidden
Figures: The Untold Story of the
African American Women Who
Helped Win the Space Race*,
HarperCollins Publishers, 2016

crgis.ndc.nasa.gov/crgis/images/d/
d3/MannBio.pdf.
Accessed 11 September, 2017

www.newscientist.com/
article/2118526-when-computers-
were-human-the-black-women-
behind-nasas-success/.
Accessed 10 September, 2017

www.washingtonpost.com/local/
hidden-no-more-katherine-
johnson-a-black-nasa-pioneer-
finds-acclaim-at-98/2017/01/27/
d6a6feb8-dd0f-11e6-ad42-
f3375f271c9c_story.html?utm_
term=.abf305e58cbd.
Accessed 12 September, 2017

Ada Lovelace (1815–1852)

Essinger, James. *A Female Genius:
How Ada Lovelace Lord Byron's
Daughter, Started the Computer
Age*, Gibson Square, 2014

Lovelace, Ada. "Translator's notes to
an article on Babbage's Analytical
Engine". *Scientific Memoirs* 3,
1842: 691–731

Morais, Betsy. "Ada Lovelace: the first
tech visionary". *The New Yorker*,
2013

Rose Dieng-Kuntz (1956–2008)

Gates Jr, Henry Louis, "Emmanuel
Akyeampong, and Steven J
Niven", in *Dictionary of African
Biography*, Oxford University
Press, 2012: 199–200

www.lemonde.fr/planete/
article/2006/01/11/
rose-dieng-un-cerveau-sans-
frontieres_729645_3244.html.
Accessed 3 September, 2017

pdfs.semanticscholar.org/5c29/610
1f7b2d0966e0903dddfb615145c
10f139.pdf.
Accessed 3 September, 2017

www.universityworldnews.com/
article.php?story=
20080717161931579.
Accessed 3 September, 2017

www.surlatoile.com/
WomenInScience/rose-dieng-
kuntz/.
Accessed 3 September, 2017

The New Historia

In creating this series, the author and publisher have worked with Gina Luria Walker, Professor of Women's Studies at The New School, New York City, and Director of The New Historia, carefully building, curating and editing the list of 48 women within this book to ensure that we uncovered as many lost female histories as possible. The New Historia's ongoing work is dedicated to the discovery, recovery, and authoritative reclamation of women of the past through time and around the globe, and honour earlier women by telling their stories and sharing their strategies that inspire us to be sturdy and brave. In them we find our foremothers, transforming and remaking our ideas about history and ourselves.

"It is imperative that we galvanize what we know so that women's legacy is acknowledged as essential to the continuum of human enlightenment. Activating what we know will also keep us from making contemporary women invisible — waiting to be brought to life 50 or 100 years from now." Gina Luria Walker, The New Historia

www.thenewhistoria.com

Allegra Lockstadt

Allegra Lockstadt was born in Canada, raised in the Southeastern United States, and currently resides in the Minneapolis, Minnesota, US. She currently works as freelance illustrator and designer. To see more of Allegra's work visit **www.allegralockstadt.com**

Sara Netherway

Sara Netherway is an illustrator from the Isle of Wight. Originally trained in fine art, she enjoys creating images with rich textures and detail. To see more of Sara's work visit **www.saranetherway.co.uk**

Lauren Simkin Berke

Lauren Simkin Berke is an American artist and illustrator based in Brooklyn, NY. Working in ink on paper, Lauren draws for clients such as *The New York Times*, *Smithsonian* magazine, Simon & Schuster publishers, and Rémy Martin.
www.simkinberke.com

Hannah Berman

Hannah Berman lives and works in Oakland, California. She loves to travel, collect bird nests and antiques, and is inspired by candy wrappers, Paint-By Numbers kits, and Islamic miniatures.

María Hergueta

María Hergueta is a freelance illustrator from a small village in north Spain. She has been working as an illustrator for five years now and her work has been published in different publishing houses and magazines such as Oxford University Press, Penguin Books, and *New York Times*.

She currently lives between Barcelona and the Swedish countryside.

Miriam Castillo

Miriam Castillo is an illustrator based in Brooklyn and Mexico. Her whimsical hand-drawn illustrations explore the intersection in between yoga, spirituality and nature. For more of her world, visit **www.miriamcastillo.com**

Marcela Quiroz

Marcela works as an illustrator for publishing projects and print media. Her day is divided between books and pencils, searching for new words, memorizing them, and writing them over and over again until they become drawings and become part of some of their alphabets of illustrated words.

www.do-re-mi.co

Shreyas Krishnan

Shreyas is an illustrator-designer from Chennai, India. She is curious about the ways in which art, design and gender intersect. Through drawing and writing, she tries to understand how, why and what we remember.

www.shreyasrkrishnan.com

Laura Inksetter

Laura Inksetter is an artist and illustrator from Ottawa, Ontario, Canada. Her work is inspired by history, folklore, and the natural world. She has a master's degree in medieval history.

Tanya Heidrich

Tanya is a Swiss, American and German graphic designer and illustrator who designs in colour, and illustrates in black and white drawing inspiration from patterns and details in everyday life.

www.tanyaheidri.ch

Winnie T Frick

Winnie T Frick is a comic artist and illustrator currently based in Brooklyn. Her interests include, cross-hatching, architecture, and dopple-gangers. Her illustrations and webcomics can be found on **www.ipsumlorum.com**

Hélène Baum

Hélène Baum is a Berlin-based illustrator. "There are no lines in nature, only areas of colour, one against another" (Manet). This principle guides her work and life. With her diverse cultural background and much traveling, she creates a cosmic space through which humour, idealism and elements from diferent cultures coexist in vibrant images.

Bodil Jane

Bodil Jane is an illustrator from Amsterdam. She graduated with honours from Willem de Kooning Academy in Rotterdam, specializing in illustration (2014). Bodil Jane loves to illustrate people, food, recipes, animals, fashion, interiors, plants, packages and maps. All of her illustrations include handmade elements and digital techniques.

pregnancy 70, 92–5
Presidential Citizen's Medal 102
Presidential Medal of Freedom 190
primatology 46–9
programming, computer
    187–201
Pterosaur 40
Pythagoras' theorem 29

Q
Qing dynasty 26, 128

R
racism, anti-Japanese 84, 86, 87
radar, plan position indicator
    (PPI) 35
radiation detection 130
radio astronomy 35–6
radioactivity
    artificial radioactivity 78–9
    beta decay 130–1
    Chien-Shiung Wu 130–1
    Lise Meitner 132, 134
    Marie Curie 76
radiology 76, 78
Radium Institute 78, 79
Raman, C V 88, 90
Ramon Magsaysay Award for
    Public Service 75
Randall, John 122
Rashtrapati Award 91
redwoods, Californian 60
relativity, theory of 128, 164
Remington Rand 189
replica plating process 58
reptiles 51–2
rhenium 118
rheumatoid arthritis 96
Rock, Margaret 161, 163
Rodríguez-Trías, Dr Helen
    99–102
Rolle theorem 76
Roosevelt, Franklin 86
Royal Astronomical Society
    31–2, 198
Royal Danish Geodetic
    Institute 20, 21
Royal Institute of Science,
    Bombay 91
Royal Navy 161, 163
Royal Observatory, Greenwich
    30–1, 32
Royal Society 186
Russell, Henry Norris 24

S
Saha, Meghnad 24
Sanger, Margaret 92–5
Sanger, William 92
sanitary napkins 182–3
satyagraha 88
Scientific American 124
Second World War (1939–45)
    anti-Japanese racism 86

Bletchley Park 120, 160–3
    conscription in US 96, 191
    CP-1 136, 138–9
    Elisabeth Kübler-Ross
        during 103–4
    French Resistance 79
    Hiroshima and Nagasaki
        130, 138–9
    Japanese occupation of the
        Philippines 74
    US declares war 86
Segrè, Emilio 130
segregation 191–2
seismology 18–21
Serapeum 154
Serapis 154
sex determination 114–15
sexual health 94–5
shingles 96
Siege of Syracuse 172
Sierra club 60
Sime, Ruth Lewin 135
Simon, Matthew 59
Simon Personal Communicator 190
smartphones 190
Smith, Mildred Davidson
    Austin 180, 183
Smithsonian's Museum of
    American History 190
snakeroot 54
Socialist Party of New York 92
Society of German Chemists 118
Sohonie, Anil 91
Sohonie, Kamala 88–91
solar eclipses 30–2
Somerville College, University
    of Oxford 147–8
Speyer School, Manhattan 110
sphygmographs 184
spiritualism 106
Squaloraja 41
Stanford University
    Esther Lederberg at 56, 59
    Nettie Stevens at 112
    Ynés Mexía at 62
stars
    classification of 14–17, 24
    composition 22, 24–5
Steinberger, Jack 131
Steiner, George 160
stereotypes 107
sterilization 101–2
Stevens, Nettie 112–15
stills 141, 178
Strassmann, Fritz 19, 135
Street, Jessie 33
street lamps 184–5
Struve, Otto 24
Suda 152
suffragettes 186
sun
    radio astronomy 35–6
    solar eclipses 30–2
    sunspots 32

surgical techniques 9, 68, 70–1
Suzhou Girls' High School 128
symmetry 167

T
Tapputi-Belatekalli 9, 140–2, 178
Tenebrio molitor 114–15
terminal illnesses 103, 104–6
Thatcher, Margaret 148
Theon 152
Theophilus 154
theory of relativity 128, 164
Thomas's formula 76
transuranium elements 119, 134
trauma, emotional 106
tree planting 64–6
tribikos 178
trigonometry 168
tungsten 116
Turing, Alan 160, 163

U
UNESCO 147
United Nations, UN Charter
    (1945) 50, 52
United States Patent and
    Trademark Office 182
University of Berlin 170
University of Bologna 144
University of California,
    Berkeley
    Chien-Shiung Wu at 130
    Leona Woods Marshall Libby
        at 139
    Ynés Mexía at 60, 62
University of Cambridge 90–1, 184
    Girton College 30
    Magdalene College 8
    Newnham College 22, 120
University of Chicago 72, 136, 139
University of Chicago Medical
    School 104
University of Cincinnati 86
University of Göttingen 164,
    166, 170
University of Heidelberg 170
University Hospital, San Juan 99
University of London, Birkbeck
    College 123
University of Michigan 98
University of Nebraska 107
University of Oxford, Somerville
    College 147–8
University of Palermo 118
University of Pittsburgh 64
University of Santo Tomas 74, 75
University of Stockholm 171
University of Sydney 33
University of Turin 124
University of Vienna 132
University of Wisconsin 56
uranium
    transuranium elements 119,
        134, 135

Acknowledgements

This book is for my mother and for all the other women in my life, but mainly my mother.
Thank you for putting up with me.

Forgotten Women would not have existed without publishing supremo Romilly Morgan,
who sought me out for a coffee and dared me to think about writing a book – then
commissioned me to write a series. I would also like to thank the team at Octopus, The
New Historia, and all the illustrators from Women Who Draw who brought these women
to life in such vivid colour. Special thanks go to Daniel Johnson and my agent Emma
Paterson of Rogers, Coleridge & White.

Zing Tsjeng

The Publisher would like to thank the entire team involved in curating the list of women
featured in *Forgotten Women: The Scientists*, and in particular would like to praise The New
Historia's ongoing work in rediscovering women's contributions throughout history.

The Publisher would also like to thank Mala Sanghera-Warren for her assistance in
researching this book.